CULTURES OF THE WORLD
Malta

Sean Sheehan and Yong Jui Lin

Marshall Cavendish
Benchmark
New York

PICTURE CREDITS

Cover: © age fotostock/SuperStock

Alamy/Photolibrary: 41, 46, 49, 66, 70, 87, 88, 91, 92, 93, 95, 97, 106, 107, 111, 112, 114, 117, 120, 122, 123, 127, 128 • alt.type/Reuters: 31, 33, 35, 36, 50 • Audrius Tomonis: 135 • Corbis: 48, 61, 69 • David Jackson: 54 • Denis Cachia: 53 • Focus Team: 8 • Francis Tan: 131 • Getty Images: 28 • Hutchison Library: 85 • Malta Tourist Office, London: 23, 27, 104 • North Wind Pictures Archives: 19, 20, 22, 76, 77, 79 • Photolibrary: 1, 3, 5, 6, 7, 9, 10, 11, 12, 14, 15, 16, 17, 18, 21, 24, 25, 26, 30, 37, 38, 39, 40, 42, 43, 44, 45, 47, 56, 57, 58, 59, 60, 62, 63, 65, 67, 68, 71, 72, 73, 74, 75, 78, 80, 81, 82, 83, 84, 86, 89, 90, 94, 96, 98, 99, 100, 102, 103, 108, 109, 110, 116, 118, 121, 124, 125, 126, 129, 130 • Spectrum photofile: 51, 52 • Topham Picturepoint: 29 • Trip Photographic Library: 13, 32, 64, 101, 105, 113 • Wikipedia: 55

PRECEDING PAGE

Bow windows on the Grand Harbour in Valletta.

Publisher (U.S.): Michelle Bisson
Editors: Deborah Grahame, Mindy Pang
Copyreader: Tara Tomczyk
Designers: Nancy Sabato, Bernard Go
Cover picture researcher: Connie Gardner
Picture researcher: Thomas Khoo

Marshall Cavendish Benchmark
99 White Plains Road
Tarrytown, NY 10591
Website: www.marshallcavendish.us

© Times Media Private Limited 2000
© Marshall Cavendish International (Asia) Private Limited 2011
® "Cultures of the World" is a registered trademark of Times Publishing Limited.

Originated and designed by Times Media Private Limited
An imprint of Marshall Cavendish International (Asia) Private Limited
A member of Times Publishing Limited

Marshall Cavendish is a trademark of Times Publishing Limited.

All Internet sites were correct and accurate at the time of printing. All monetary figures in this publication are in U.S. dollars.

Library of Congress Cataloging-in-Publication Data
Sheehan, Sean.
 Malta / Sean Sheehan and Yong Jui Lin. — 2nd ed.
  p. cm. — (Cultures of the world)
 Includes bibliographical references and index.
 Summary: "Provides comprehensive information on the geography, history,
  wildlife, governmental structure, economy, cultural diversity, peoples,
  religion, and culture of Malta"—Provided by publisher.
 ISBN 978-1-60870-024-0
 1. Malta—Juvenile literature. I. Yong Jui Lin. II. Title.
 F2368.5.J47 2010
 988.1—dc22   2010000724

Printed in China
7 6 5 4 3 2 1

CONTENTS

INTRODUCTION

MALTA, A SMALL ARCHIPELAGO IN THE CENTER OF THE Mediterranean Sea, has attracted foreign cultures from time immemorial, with its megalithic temples that bear testimony to more than 6,000 years of human history. Beginning with ancient, unknown migrants from neighboring lands in the Mediterranean, and continuing apace with the crowds of tourists that now invade the islands every year, Malta has managed to preserve its culture remarkably well. This is borne out by the Maltese language, which continues to thrive among a people who number well below half a million. The durability of its national tongue is just one example of Malta's resilience. This book introduces many other aspects of this small European culture that maintains its independence with dignity and fortitude. As Europe grows closer together, economically and politically, Malta shows how a minority culture can avoid becoming an endangered one.

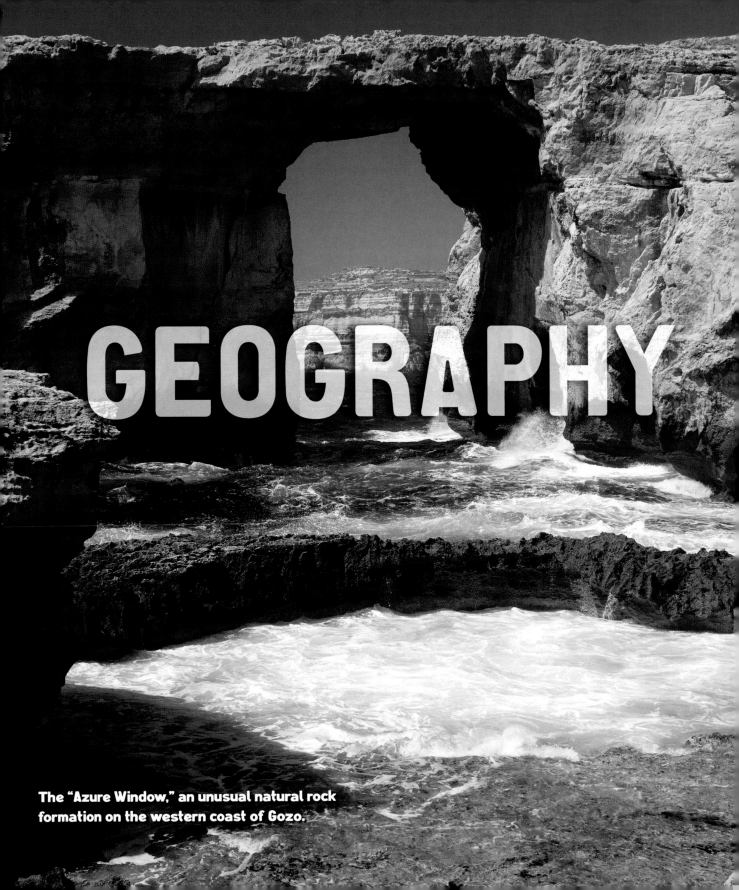

GEOGRAPHY

The "Azure Window," an unusual natural rock formation on the western coast of Gozo.

MALTA CONSISTS OF THREE MAIN islands—the island of Malta itself, the smaller island of Gozo, and tiny Comino. Cominotto, Filfla, and Saint Paul's Islands are large rocks that help make up the Maltese archipelago. All the islands lie midway between Gibraltar, at the western end of the Mediterranean Sea, and Lebanon at the eastern end.

The islands of Malta cover an area of 122 square miles (316 square kilometers).

The coast of Comino with its beautiful blue lagoon.

To the north lies the island of Sicily, 58 miles (93 kilometers) away, while 220 miles (354 km) to the south lies Tripoli, the seaport capital of Libya. Malta is located in the center of the Mediterranean, midway between Europe and North Africa.

The largest island, Malta, is 17 miles (27 km) long and 9 miles (14 km) wide and covers an area of 95 square miles (246 square km). Gozo is only 9 miles (14 km) long by 5 miles (8 km) wide, with an area of 26 square miles (67 square km), while Comino has an area of only one square mile (2.6 square km). A channel of water 3 miles (5 km) wide separates Malta and Gozo, and Comino lies between them.

TERRAIN

The south of Malta
is not Europe's
southernmost point;
this distinction be-
longs to the Greek
island of Gavdos.

The three main islands are mostly composed of limestone and rise to a maximum height of just over 829 feet (253 meters) at the Dingli Cliffs in the southwest of Malta island. However, the land is not as flat as this might suggest, as there are lots of escarpments, or steep slopes at the edge of an area of level ground that drop into a narrow valley.

One of the most prominent escarpments is the Mdina-Verdala Ridge, where the Dingli Cliffs are situated. To the north of the ridge, separated by small hills, is an array of narrow valleys that make their way down to the coast. These lower-lying areas have good alluvial soils and are cultivated with the help of irrigation.

Malta's terrain is mostly rocky and sparse, devoid of mountains and rivers and with little vegetation, although there are many small fields enclosed by stone walls. Between February and March, Malta is briefly transformed into myriads of colors when tulips, crocuses, and other flowers brighten up the otherwise barren countryside. The island of Gozo, thanks to the high clay content of its soil, has a more verdant landscape.

The coastlines of the main islands are well indented and there are countless small harbors, creeks, bays, and sandy coves. The Grand Harbour in Valletta is a natural deep-water harbor 80 feet (24 m) deep and has been of great economic as well as strategic importance for thousands of years. The total length of the shoreline around Malta island is 84 miles (135 km), and 27 miles (43 km) around Gozo.

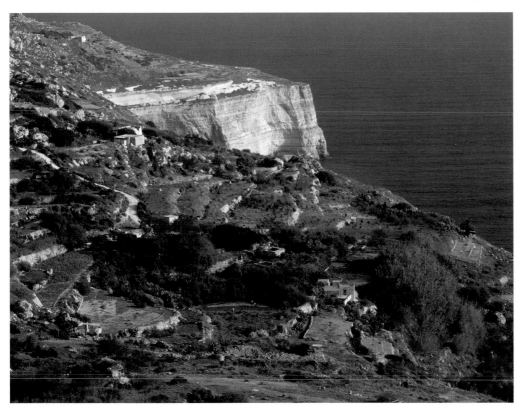

The Dingli Cliffs in South Malta.

FLOWERS

Malta is not a place usually associated with colorful flowers. This is partly because the flowering season lasts only a couple of months and partly because the soil and the climate do not encourage a rich variety of plants. What does flourish is a giant clover, called the sulla, which produces a purple-colored flower. Because farmers use it as a fodder crop, its growth is encouraged.

Shrubs that flower are cultivated for ornamental purposes along roads and at other public places. These include the pink-and-white oleander, the orange-colored lantana, the geranium, and the bougainvillea. Some of these shrubs are also nurtured in pots by families who like to add some color to the exterior of their homes by placing painted or pottery containers against an outside wall. Apartment-dwellers often like to cultivate flowering shrubs that hang down from their balconies. Even in very arid areas, the ubiquitous prickly pear (opuntia), a type of cactus, bears a yellow flower in fall.

The famous Maltese falcon, the title of one of Hollywood's most memorable black-and-white movies, is the Mediterranean peregrine falcon. It used to nest under cliffs on Gozo island, but sadly became a protected species too late to save it from extinction in the mid-1980s. The same fate befell the Mediterranean sea eagle—another victim of the peculiar "hobby" of killing birds that is now banned in Malta.

The squirting cucumber, or faqqus il-hmir *(FAT-ous ill-hmeer), may not be as well known as the Maltese falcon, but it is thriving and is in no danger of extinction, thanks perhaps to its peculiar form of propagation. The seeds of most plants are usually spread by bees, animals, or the wind, but the* faqqus il-hmir *is able to eject its seeds with enough force to propel them to some distance away from the plant. The seeds are formed in a liquid-filled fruit that dramatically explodes when ripe, thus spreading the seeds. The* faqqus il-hmir *is a very common plant in Malta and grows on wasteland.*

FAUNA AND FLORA

Malta does not have a great variety of wildlife. The shortage of water, combined with the poor quality of the soil, has resulted in the Mediterranean shrub being the only natural vegetation. The mammals that are able to survive are mostly small animals, such as hedgehogs, weasels, and shrews. Resident birds include the Manx and Cory's shearwaters, the blue rock thrush, and the Sardinian warbler. During spring and fall, Malta is visited by countless thousands of migrating birds, and the shooting of these birds has recently stopped being a popular leisure activity for some Maltese.

Above: **Pretty poppies growing in Malta.**

Opposite: **The fertile Ramla Valley in Gozo.**

The Judas tree (*Cercis siliquastrum*) is common. It gets its name from the legend that it was the kind of tree from which Judas Iscariot, an apostle of Jesus Christ, hanged himself after betraying Jesus. At one time oak trees covered the islands, but most have long since been cut down. Only a few small pockets of these indigenous trees remain.

What has survived in more plentiful numbers is the carob or algarroba (*Ceratonia siliqua*), also known as the locust tree, which derives its name from a biblical legend associated with both John the Baptist and the prodigal son. The pods are edible, and although now mainly used to feed cattle, they were once a source of food for hungry peasants. The juice from the pods was also used to make drinks and syrups. Other trees that are able to survive Malta's hot and dry climate include the fig, the sweet bay, and the almond.

Date palms, imported from North Africa, are a common sight. Also found in Malta are orange trees, which were also introduced to the islands. Malta has more than 600 species of wildflowers.

CLIMATE

Summers in Malta are long, hot, and dry. Winters are mild and snowfall is unknown. Although the average yearly rainfall is 24 inches (61 centimeters), it rarely rains during the summer months. The average temperature between April and October is 79.2°F (26.2°C), although temperatures may rise to 96°F (36°C). In the winter months, from November to March, the average temperature is 62.2°F (16.8°C).

This typical Mediterranean combination of a long and hot summer with a dry and mild winter is ideal for attracting tourists from colder climates. Not

A LAND WITHOUT RIVERS

Malta has no rivers. In the past this meant complete dependence on water from wells. Small, privately owned windmills are a common sight in the countryside, where they are used to power wells to irrigate farm land. The government has built many reservoirs, and there are also a number of desalination plants, which extract salt from sea water before it is pumped into a reservoir.

Water is also pumped up from natural underground hollows in the rock where rainwater that has percolated through the soil collects. Malta depends on underground reserves of fresh water, drawn through a system of water tunnels called the Ta' Kandja galleries, which average about 318 feet (97 m) below the surface and extend like the spokes of a wheel. Drilling a well to reach the water is no longer a problem with modern technology. Desalination plants account for over 60 percent of the water used on the island and, although expensive, has relieved the shortage of fresh water.

surprisingly Malta is very popular with visitors year-round. Moreover, because no place in Malta is more than a few miles from the sea, sea breezes help moderate the heat of the summer months. The best known of these cooling winds is the *gregale* (grey-GAH-lay), which blows in from high altitudes in southern Italy and Sicily. The *gregale* can last up to three days and is feared by fishermen because of its ability to whip up waves and endanger small craft.

In early summer and again at the end of the summer, a warm and sultry wind blows in from the Sahara Desert in Africa. Some people believe the wind, called the scirocco, affects their temperament, causing them to become annoyed by small matters that would not normally bother them.

URBAN CENTERS

Although Valletta is the capital of Malta, it is not the largest town. The city proper has a population of 6,315, compared with the towns of Birkirkara and Qormi, which have more than three times that number of people. More than 20,000 people live in Sliema, a prosperous middle-class district on Malta island. Sliema, situated close to Valletta, is home to the fashionable Tower Road, where boutiques and other upscale shops adjoin blocks of luxurious apartments.

The original capital of Malta was Mdina, an inland town. The site of this fortified city was well chosen—a high precipice on a ridge that was easy to defend. But when the Knights of Saint John arrived in the 16th century, they preferred a base closer to the coast. When the Great Siege of 1565 ended, the Knights committed themselves to making Malta their permanent home and built a new capital that could hold a commanding position over the main harbor. The capital was named after the leader of the Knights, the Grand Master Jean Parisot de la Valette, who had led them to their great victory over the Turks.

LIFE IN THE SEA

The Mediterranean Sea has some of the most polluted waters in the world and this has affected the diversity of the sea life around Malta. There are several varieties of mackerel as well as red mullet, bass, and skate. Local fish popular in restaurants and Maltese kitchens include dentici *(den-TEE-chee),* lampuka *(lam-POO-ka), and* pixxixspad *(pish-SHISH-pad).*

The small fishing industry uses traditional Maltese fishing boats, called luzzijiet *(LUT-tsie-yiet), which are a familiar sight at small harbors around Malta and Gozo. As in other Mediterranean cultures, there is a lively tradition of painting boats in bright colors and adding an image of a large eye on either side of the prow.*

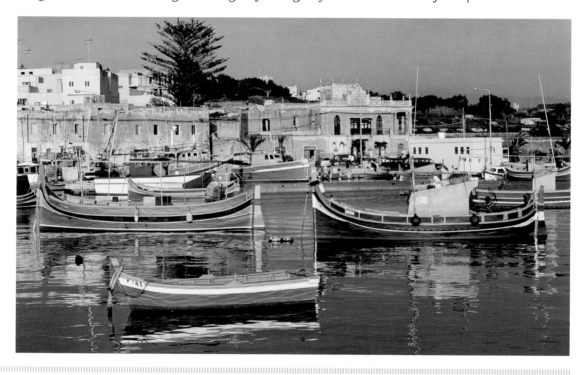

The largest town in Gozo is Victoria. Its original name, and one by which it is sometimes still identified, is Rabat (meaning "the town"), but this was changed by the British in 1897 in honor of Queen Victoria. Unlike many other countries colonized by the British, the Maltese have not felt the need to assert their independence by removing linguistic markers of imperial rule.

HISTORY

A memorial in Palace Square in Valletta
commemorates the 1919 riots that led to greater
self-government for the Maltese under British rule.

VII GUNJU 1919

M
ALTA HAS JUSTLY BEEN LABELED the cradle of Mediterranean culture because of its many megaliths that date back to the dawn of European civilization. More generally the history of Malta can be seen to encapsulate European history as a whole. It began with the first arrival of nomadic peoples from Sicily in the north some 7,000 years ago.

Jean Parisot de la Valette, who led the Knights of Malta to their great victory over the Turks in 1565, is one of the most famous people in Malta's long history. He joined the Order of Saint John at the age of 20 and was elected Grand Master in 1557, at the age of 63. His tomb in the church of Saint John in Valletta bears an inscription commemorating "the scourge of Africa and Asia and the shield of Europe."

The Tarxien temples southeast of Valletta are among the best preserved Neolithic structures in Malta.

One of the most notable periods of Malta's history is the Temple period, starting around 3,600 B.C. The Ggantia Prehistoric Temples in Gozo are the oldest freestanding buildings in the world. Many of the temples are in the form of five semicircular rooms connected at the center. It has been suggested that these might have represented the head, arms, and legs of a deity, since one of the most common kinds of statue found in these temples is a fat woman—a symbol of fertility. The Temple period lasted until about 2,500 B.C., at which point the civilization that raised these huge monoliths seems to have disappeared. There is much speculation about what might have happened and whether they were completely wiped out or assimilated.

The Neolithic cave-dwellers who built the megaliths were followed by a Bronze Age society. Then came a succession of more powerful cultures—Carthaginians, Romans, Arabs, Normans, the Knights of Saint John, the French, and then the British at the turn of the 19th century. Finally, the Maltese gained their independence in 1964.

TEMPLE BUILDERS

The earliest inhabitants were Stone Age people who are thought to have first arrived in Malta around 5000 B.C. Although they lacked knowledge of metals, they used their expertise with stone to leave a permanent reminder of their presence on Malta. Around the same time that the Egyptians first began building pyramids, the Neolithic Maltese began constructing impressive megalithic temples on Gozo and Malta.

Some of the most famous temples, such as the Tarxien (tar-SHEEN) temple and the Hypogeum of Hal Saflieni, were only discovered by accident in the early 20th century. Tarxien was uncovered when a farmer plowing his field kept blunting his plow on large stones just under the soil. Later, excavations revealed a temple complex and important prehistoric works of art. The Hypogeum, a vast underground chamber cut from rock and later used as a burial chamber, was discovered by a builder working on the foundations for a house he was building.

The ancient Greeks, impressed by the sweet product of the bees on Malta, named the islands Melita (meaning "honey").

PHOENICIANS AND CARTHAGINIANS

The influence of the Phoenicians and the Carthaginians was felt from around 1500 B.C. to 216 B.C. The Phoenicians, a Bronze Age maritime power based in what is now Lebanon in the eastern Mediterranean, used Malta as a staging post as they sailed from one end of the Mediterranean to the other. They also established a colony at Carthage, in what is now Tunisia in North Africa. The Carthaginians developed their own power base after Phoenicia declined in importance.

The Phoenicians dominated trade in the Mediterranean some 3,000 years ago. Tombs have been uncovered in Malta, suggesting that some Phoenicians settled on the islands.

A small number of Phoenician inscriptions have been found in Malta and, being a Semitic language, it was believed for a long time that Maltese was Phoenician in origin. The Carthaginians also used Malta as a base, and although there is little archaeological evidence of their presence, their influence lives on in the popular Maltese name, Nibblu, which is a shortened form of Hannibal, the most famous Carthaginian in history. After a fierce struggle against the power of Rome, Carthage was finally destroyed. For Malta this heralded a long period of rule under the Romans.

THE ROMANS

Rome, which held undisputed power over the entire Mediterranean region, paid little attention to Malta even though the islands were under Roman influence for some 800 years. The Romans first arrived during the Second Punic War (218—201 B.C.) between Rome and Carthage, and Malta fell under the responsibility of the Roman governor of Sicily.

Malta became an outpost of the Roman Empire after the Carthaginians were defeated in the Second Punic War.

In A.D. 60 a ship heading for Rome was shipwrecked off the coast of Malta. There were well over 200 passengers on board. One of them, Saint Paul, remained on the island for three months and converted the Roman governor, Publius. This is how Christianity is believed to have come to Malta, which was one of the earliest Roman colonies to be Christianized. Today the annual celebration of his shipwreck is still an important event. If the tradition is true, then the Maltese were one of the first non-Jewish people to convert to the new religion.

THE ARABS

The islands of Malta were conquered by the Arabs in A.D. 870. The new invaders would retain control until the arrival of the Normans 220 years later. Not a great deal is known about how Malta was governed during this period because the conquerors regarded these small islands as only a tiny part of a vast area of influence that spread from Spain in the west, across the Mediterranean and including Sicily, to the Indus River in the east.

Malta, as in the days of Roman rule, was only a province of Sicily. Nevertheless the short period of Arab conquest had a lasting effect on the language that developed into the Maltese that is spoken today. The introduction of citrus fruits and cotton to Malta is also attributed to the Arabs. The Arabs built their fortified capital, which they named Mdina, on the site of the old Roman capital.

Although they introduced their language to the islanders, they did not convert the people to Islam and so Christianity retained its influence over the lives of the people of Malta.

During Arab rule, the walled city of Mdina was the capital of Malta.

THE NORMANS

The Normans, a mixed race of people from Normandy in France, conquered large parts of the Mediterranean in the 11th century, including Sicily. In 1090 they arrived from Sicily and began to displace the Arabs as rulers of Malta. The Arabs living on Malta did not resist the Normans by force, and Muslims continued to live there as they had done before. It was not until 1224 that the Muslims were expelled from the islands.

Unlike the Romans, the various Norman rulers who governed Malta failed to contain the major problem of marauding pirates from North Africa. Known as corsairs, the pirates found Malta to be a useful watering hole and base for mounting attacks on passing shipping. As a result, Malta never endeared itself to the European powers, especially after a raid in 1525 that led to 400 people of various ranks and nationalities being captured and either enslaved or held for ransom. By this time Malta had passed into the hands of the Spanish emperor, Charles V, and he offered it to the Knights of Saint John, who were anxiously looking for a new home.

In 1530 Charles V granted Malta to the homeless Knights of Saint John, who then ruled the islands for over 250 years.

THE ORDER OF SAINT JOHN

The year 1530 is very significant in Malta's history because this was when the Knights of the Order of Saint John first arrived on the islands. The order exercised political and economic control over the islands. The police, the legal system, and even the water supply were all controlled by the order, and all the key positions in the administration of Malta were held by Knights. The

A tapestry depicting the Great Siege of 1565. The anniversary of the ending of the siege on September 8 is one of the most important public holidays in Malta.

local population, which numbered around 12,000 in 1530, had little contact with the Knights, but they were subject to them, and thanks to the Order's control of the police and military garrisons, the population had little choice but to accept their authority.

THE GREAT SIEGE

The Knights had little interest in an inland capital like Mdina so they set about building new bases on the coast. In May 1565 a huge fleet of Turkish ships with 40,000 men arrived, aiming to completely destroy the Knights. It took them a month to take Fort Saint Elmo, but the Knights in Fort Saint Angelo managed to hold out against a total surrender of the island. In September, when Christian reinforcements began to arrive, the Turks sailed away and the Great Siege was over. The Great Siege has entered Maltese history as one of the nation's great defining moments. The Knights' Grand Master, Jean Parisot de la Valette, survived the siege with just 600 men, while the leader of the Ottomans, Dragut, died in the fighting.

The Order of Saint John was first established in the late 11th century as the Hospitallers, a group of monks who set out to provide medical care for Christian pilgrims traveling to the Holy Land. However, the Holy Land is also holy to Islam, and this brought the pilgrims into conflict with the Arabs and created a need for a military force capable of protecting the pilgrims. In this way, the Hospitallers evolved into an order of Christian Knights, drawn from the aristocratic families of Europe, who were committed to vows of celibacy, poverty, and obedience to their grand master. As Islam grew more powerful, the Knights were expelled from the Holy Land. They established a base on the island of Rhodes, off the coast of Greece. From there they could sail out to attack the enemy.

The Knights became pirates in their own way, taking every opportunity to attack Turkish merchants and rob their ships. The advance of Islam, driven by the Ottoman Empire, led to the expulsion of the Knights from Rhodes. After eight years of wandering around Europe seeking a home, they were granted the island of Malta in 1530.

The grand master, the most important rank in the order, was the official head of the Knights. The Knights adopted the distinctive eight-pointed cross, known as the Maltese Cross, as their emblem. Each of the eight points of the cross represents one of the beatitudes given in Christ's Sermon on the Mount, while the four main sections represent the Christian virtues of fortitude, justice, temperance, and prudence.

AFTER THE SIEGE

The Knights were determined to secure their island home against any future attack, so work soon began on the building of Valletta. The town took five years to complete, gave the Knights a secure home for more than 200 years, and heralded an age of prosperity for Malta. By the mid-18th century, however, the Turkish Ottoman Empire was in decline and no longer posed a threat. The rule of the Knights came to an end in 1798 when Napoleon Bonaparte of France captured Malta and confiscated all their land and property. The revolutionary and anticlerical French army also abolished the Maltese nobility.

A painting of Malta's harbor in 1812.

But by attacking the Church, the French made many enemies. When Napoleon set off for Egypt he left only a small force behind. When the Maltese rose in rebellion, the French were taken by surprise. They managed to hold out in Valletta until 1800 but finally surrendered and Malta fell into the hands of France's enemy at the time, the British.

BRITISH RULE

At first the British did not realize the strategic importance of their new acquisition, but in time they grew to appreciate the usefulness of controlling a small group of islands in the middle of the Mediterranean, especially after the opening of the Suez Canal in 1869.

After World War I, popular demonstrations calling for the Maltese to have a greater say in the running of their country were held. In 1919 four Maltese were shot dead by British troops during a demonstration. Later the same year the British announced plans to draw up a more liberal constitution. The new constitution left power over important matters such as defense and immigration in the hands of the British, but also created a Maltese government with an elected assembly to govern many other aspects of life. This system

Before the arrival of the British, the official language since 1530 (and the one of the educated elite) had been Italian, but this was downgraded by the increased use of English. In 1934 English and Maltese were declared the sole official languages.

worked well until 1933, when the British suspended the Maltese government because it disapproved of its attempts to reintroduce Italian as the language of instruction in schools, instead of English. For the next 14 years, the Maltese government remained suspended.

WORLD WAR II

The strategic importance of Malta in any struggle for control of the Mediterranean became obvious during World War II. Several German generals called for an invasion of the island because as long as it remained in British hands, enemy planes and submarines would be able to use it as a base. This would allow the British to attack the German convoys that were supplying their troops in the war in North Africa.

Adolf Hitler, however, preferred to launch an aerial attack and planned to bomb and starve Malta into submission by subjecting it to a second great siege. The island became one of the most heavily bombed targets during World War II. In two months in 1942, for example, more bombs were dropped

A painting depicting the Grand Harbour in Malta under air attack during World War II. Despite heavy bombing by German forces during World War II, Malta managed to hold out.

on Malta than on all of London in a year. Many families moved to Gozo, where there was only a single small runway to attract the attention of enemy planes.

As essential supplies dwindled, it seemed almost certain that Malta would be forced to surrender. Everything came to depend on a convoy of 14 supply ships, escorted by battleships, aircraft carriers, cruisers, and destroyers, which set out on a final rescue mission in 1942. The convoy was an easy target for enemy planes and submarines, and the attempt to reach Malta became a dramatic journey through a corridor of bombs and torpedoes. When the *Ohio*, the first of the five supply ships that survived, was finally towed into Grand Harbour, it was met by cheering crowds and tears of relief.

INDEPENDENCE

In the first general election after World War II, Malta got its first Labor government. In 1955 Dominic Mintoff became the leader of the Labour Party. A charismatic and controversial politician, Mintoff led Malta's demands for full independence from Britain, which was finally achieved in 1964. The main difficulties facing the country were economic, a major setback being Britain's decision to cut its own defense budget by abandoning expensive overseas bases. In Malta, where the British employed about one in five of Malta's working population in the British-owned local dockyards, this forced the country to look to its own future. In 1979 the British military base in Malta was finally closed, and the last of the British forces sailed away from the islands for the last time. Malta was now truly independent and entirely responsible for its own affairs.

In the same year, the first overtures were made to the European Economic Community (now called the Economic Union, or EU), and in 1990 a formal application to join the EU was submitted. A referendum on the EU membership in 2003 saw a majority of over 19,000 votes in favor of membership from 91 percent of those who had the right to vote, and Malta joined the EU in May 1, 2004. On January 1, 2008, Malta adopted the euro, the currency of the EU.

The citation of April 1942 from George VI of England, when Malta received Britain's highest possible civilian award for exceptional courage-the George Cross. This honor was never before-or since-awarded to an entire country.

A FAMOUS FACE OF MALTA

Dominic (Dom) Mintoff was born in 1916 into a poor family and at a time when Malta, as just one of Britain's many overseas territories, had very little control over its own affairs. He trained as a civil engineer but became more interested in politics. He helped organize the Labour Party's first electoral victory in 1947 before going on to become the leader of the party. He was prime minister four times before finally stepping down in 1984.

Dom Mintoff became the best-known Maltese politician internationally, mainly due to his relationship with Britain. At one point Mintoff was so pro-British that he suggested Malta should become an integral part of the United Kingdom itself. When this was rejected by Britain, his own position changed, and he later led the demands for full independence.

Dom Mintoff is equally famous for his battles with the Catholic Church in Malta. He dared to openly criticize the Church for its authoritarianism and for its great wealth. He attempted to confiscate Church property and limit the political influence of priests. As a socialist, he struggled to improve the quality of life for the ordinary citizens of Malta, and in this respect, he achieved a great deal. Many important improvements, such as the introduction of free higher education, were due to his efforts. He is still revered by many Maltese. No other politician, before or since his time, has achieved so much for Malta.

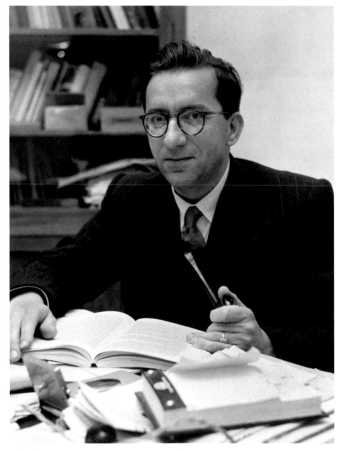

MODERN-DAY KNIGHTS

Two hundred years after their expulsion from Malta by Napoleon's troops, the Knights of Saint John made a triumphant return when they were granted a 99-year lease on Fort Saint Angelo in 1998. The fort was the scene of their greatest victory in 1565, when some 600 Knights and 8,000 Maltese soldiers stemmed the tide of Muslim expansionism by successfully holding out against 40,000 Turks and their armada of 300 ships.

Today the order is known as the Sovereign Military Hospitaller Order of Saint John of Jerusalem, of Rhodes, and of Malta (known as the Sovereign Military Order of Malta—SMOM, or the Order of Malta or Knights of Malta for short). It is a Roman Catholic order based in Rome, Italy, and a sovereign subject of international law. The order currently has 12,500 members, 80,000 permanent volunteers, and 20,000 medical personnel, including doctors, nurses, auxiliaries and paramedics. The goal is to assist the elderly, the handicapped, refugees, children, the homeless, and those with terminal illness and leprosy in five continents of the world, without distinction of race or religion. Through its worldwide relief corps, Malteser International, the Order also aids victims of natural disasters, epidemics, and armed conflicts.

GOVERNMENT

The prime minister's office in Valletta.

CHAPTER 3

F ULL DEMOCRACY CAME LATE to Malta. During the 20th century the British granted various limited forms of representative government to the Maltese, but whenever these governments reached decisions that were unpalatable to the British, they were simply removed. This happened several times—in 1903, 1930, 1933, and 1958.

Malta has the second-highest voter turnout in the world (and the highest for nations without mandatory voting), based on election turnout in national lower house elections from 1960 to 1995.

Crowds of people celebrating in Floriana outside Valletta after Malta's ruling Nationalist Party won a third consecutive term during the 2008 general elections.

British and Russian ships docked at a Maltese port.

Nevertheless Malta has enjoyed a free press from as early as 1839, and voting by secret ballot has been the practice since 1849, when the country's first constitution, which gave the Maltese little say in political matters, was promulgated. When the country finally achieved control over its own affairs in the early 1960s, the Maltese people were more than ready to take over the reins of power.

THE CONSTITUTION

Malta became an independent state on September 21, 1964, following a system of parliamentary democracy based on regular elections and universal suffrage. Until December, 13, 1974, when the country became a republic, Malta still recognized the British monarch, and a governor-general representing the crown lived in Valletta. Today the head of state is the president. Although the president appoints the prime minister and the leader of the opposition, he or she does not hold political power. Executive power rests with the prime minister, who chooses a cabinet of ministers to govern the country.

Malta remains a member of the Commonwealth and foreign policy is governed by a commitment to neutrality. The constitution does not allow the country to join a military alliance or allow foreign military bases on its territory.

The Cold War was formally ended at the December 1989 summit meeting in Malta between U.S. president George H. W. Bush and Soviet president Mikhail Gorbachev.

THE PARTY SYSTEM

The first political parties were formed at the end of the 19th century when the educated elite, unhappy with plans by the British to promote the English language at the expense of Italian, began to organize an opposition. The Nationalist Party developed from this pro-Italian group, while another group, supporting the promotion of English, became the Constitutional Party in the 1920s.

Today Maltese politics is dominated by two main parties—the Nationalist Party and the Labour Party. There are 69 members in the Maltese parliament.

The Labour Party was once able to command a majority of seats in the House of Representatives, even though it received a smaller number of total votes than the Nationalist Party. As a result election rules were changed in the 1990s so that whichever party gains an absolute majority of votes will form the new government, even if this means creating additional seats in parliament. However, the Labour Party has accused the Nationalists of having engineered a built-in electoral advantage because of the way they have divided up the electoral areas.

The Nationalist government wrapped up negotiations for European Union (EU) membership by the end of 2002. A referendum on the issue was called in March 2003 for which the Nationalists campaigned for a "yes" vote while Labor campaigned heavily for a "no" vote. Turnout was 91 percent, with more than 53 percent voting "yes." On May 1, 2004, Malta joined the EU and on January 1, 2008, the Eurozone, with the euro as the national currency. The first elections after membership were held in March 2008, resulting in a narrow victory for the Nationalist Party with 49.34 percent of first-preference votes.

Although many Maltese would forcefully argue against the idea, the difference between the two parties is not enormous. Though the differences between the parties may seem insignificant to outsiders, this does not mean that political debate is muted. The opposite is often the case, and politics remains a divisive and highly passionate affair for many Maltese.

Malta Labour Party supporters cheer party leader Sant at a party mass meeting in Pembroke.

If the United States had the same proportion of representatives as Malta, roughly one to 500 people, there would be 50,000 members of Congress!

SYMBOLS OF THE STATE

The Emblem

The emblem of Malta consists of a shield that carries a heraldic image of the national flag. At the top is a gold crown with a sally port and eight turrets (although only five are visible). These represent the fortifications of Malta. Around the shield is a wreath of olive leaves on one side and a palm frond on the other, both symbols of peace that are traditionally associated with the country. At the bottom of the wreath is a white ribbon with the words Repubblika ta' Malta *(Republic of Malta).*

The National Flag

The national flag of Malta consists of two equal vertical stripes of white and red. A representation of the George Cross, awarded to Malta in 1942 in recognition of the islands' tremendous bravery in World War II, appears in the top left-hand corner of the white stripe. Tradition has it that the white and red colors were awarded to Malta by Count Roger I, the Norman ruler of Sicily, in appreciation for the hospitality shown him in 1090 when he ousted the Arabs.

There is also a maritime flag of Malta. This consists of a red field bordered in white and bearing a Maltese cross in white in the center.

The National Anthem

The music for Malta's national anthem was composed before the lyrics were written. The music was given to a well-known priest-poet, Dun Karm, in the early 1920s to write a school hymn. He used the music to write a prayer that would unite the different political opinions of the Maltese. In 1945 it became the official national anthem:

> *Guard her, O Lord, as ever Thou hast guarded!*
> *This Motherland so dear whose name as bear!*
> *Keep her in mind, whom Thou hast made so fair!*
> *May he who rules, for wisdom be regarded!*
> *In master mercy, strength in man increase!*
> *Confirm us all, in unity and peace!*

One of the first major issues to divide the people of Malta politically was the power of the Catholic Church in the running of the country. The government that took power after the 1927 elections, led by the Constitutional Party, argued that the clergy should not take part in politics. At the time priests were members of the new assembly. The issue became a bitter controversy that lasted for many years. The elections scheduled for 1930 were suspended after the Church instructed people not to vote for the Constitutional Party. A similar controversy erupted when a Labour government under Dom Mintoff was elected in 1955. The Labour Party's reluctance to yield to the Church led to an ongoing bitter dispute.

A STILL-POWERFUL CHURCH

The Catholic Church in Malta has a long tradition of playing a decisive role in the government of the country. For centuries before there was any democratic government, the majority of people looked to their local church for guidance on nonspiritual as well as religious matters. After the British first introduced a very limited form of self-government people continued to turn to their priests for advice. At the same time, the Church was eager to ensure that its power and influence would not be eroded by support for secular politicians.

Problems arose when disagreements between the Church and the Labour Party began. In the 1950s and 1960s matters came to a head when Dom Mintoff confronted the political power and ambitions of the Church. In the 1962 election, the Church told the people of Malta, who were overwhelmingly Catholic, that it would be a sin to vote for the Labour Party and that even reading a Labour Party newspaper was against God's wishes. The opposition Nationalist Party won the 1962 election and was reelected in 1966 when the Church again sided with the Nationalist Party and warned people not to vote for the Labour Party.

Matthew Festing, Grand Master of the Order of Malta, with Pope Benedict XVI.

When the Labour Party formed the government in 1955, it tried to limit the power of the Church by subjecting it to taxation and by removing the immunity of the archbishop and bishops from the authority of the criminal and civil courts. Attempts to limit the power of the Church in education were less successful and serve as a reminder that the Church is still a powerful force in Maltese politics.

POLITICS TODAY

In 1996 a Labour government was formed after a decade of Nationalist rule but with a majority of only one seat. This slender majority, combined with infighting within the Labour Party, led to a snap election on September 5, 1998. The Nationalists won and Eddie Fenech-Adami became the prime minister. In the general elections in 2002 the Nationalists returned to office with 51.79 percent of the vote against the Labour's 47.51 percent. This was seen as an endorsement of the Nationalists pro-EU stance. Fenech-Adami (born in 1934) succeeded to the leadership of his party in 1977. He had led the Nationalists to victory in previous elections. Lawrence Gonzi became prime minister on March 23, 2004, following the resignation of Fenech-Adami, and was reconfirmed on March 10, 2008, after another Nationalist victory at the polls on March 8, 2008.

Nationalist Party leader and reelected prime minister Gonzi meets his supporters.

In the past, whenever a new government was formed, one of the first tasks of the new political leadership was to appoint party supporters to important positions in all the government departments and state-owned companies, such as the banks and the national airline. This practice has not been implemented for some time, perhaps a sign that Malta's politics are falling more in line with that of other European nations, aiming to be transparent and above-board.

The law courts in Valletta. The Maltese police, the *pulizija* (PULL-IT-see-ya), are an unarmed force. The blue uniform of its officers is another legacy of British rule.

THE JUDICIARY

The term *judiciary* refers to the system in which judges administer justice in a country. One of the central features of democratic countries is that the judiciary remains separate from the executive, which is the part of the country's system of government that holds political power and makes decisions as a result of having that power.

In Malta judges and magistrates are appointed by the president and cannot be removed from office just because a different party gains power or because the government disagrees with a judgment of the courts. There is also a special Constitutional Court that decides on matters arising from the constitution and on matters relating to human rights. Maltese law follows the principle common to American and British justice that a person's guilt, not innocence, has to be proven in court.

ECONOMY

A fisherman unknotting his fishing net in Marsaxlokk.

CHAPTER 4

MALTA PRODUCES ONLY ABOUT 20 percent of the food it needs, has limited supplies of fresh water, and has few domestic energy sources. Malta's geographic position between the EU and Africa makes it a common destination for illegal immigrants, and this has strained Malta's political and economic resources.

Salt pans at the coast near Marsalforn on Gozo island.

Malta's economy is dependent on foreign trade, manufacturing—especially electronics and pharmaceuticals—and tourism, all of which were negatively affected by the global economic downturn in 2009. The good news is that economic recovery of the European economy has lifted exports, tourism, and overall growth. Malta adopted the euro on January 1, 2008. The Maltese government in 2009 was challenged to contain the budget deficit, which ballooned in 2008 to about 4.7 percent of GDP, placing it above the Eurozone's 3 percent maximum.

THE GROSS DOMESTIC PRODUCT

The gross domestic product (GDP) is the total value of goods and services produced by a country over a set period, usually a year. For Malta the GDP averages about $24,200 per person. One of the largest contributions to the GDP comes from manufacturing. In the past this sector was dominated by the clothing and textile industries. Today, however, the electronics industry

Quarry workers on the job. Most of Malta's limestone is used in the local construction industry.

is becoming increasingly important. The government offers various tax concessions and other financial benefits to encourage companies to set up businesses in Malta, and this is proving very successful. Another significant manufacturing activity is the ship-repair industry. This is a more traditional part of Malta's economy and originated in the days when Britain maintained dockyards to service its navy and commercial fleets. About one-quarter of Malta's working population is employed in manufacturing.

A woman making lace in a lace factory in Gozo. Malta is renowned for its delicate lace.

The single largest contribution to the GDP comes from tourism and other services. The growing number of visitors, now more than a million a year, makes tourism a crucial part of the country's economy. In 2003, 1.2 million tourists visited the island. The government's success in promoting Malta as an international business center has also contributed significantly to Malta's economy.

TOURISM

Tourism is a major earner of foreign currency, and any sudden decline in the number of visitors would be disastrous for the economy. Tourism accounts for 35 percent of GDP, and government policy aims to further increase this figure. Britain accounts for just under half the total number of visitors, followed by Germany and Italy. Lace-making is a traditional handicraft in Malta that has been harnessed to the tourist market. There are no factories, as this is still a home-based industry practiced entirely by women whose hand-crocheted work is now applied to far more than lace. Blouses, skirts, and shawls are painstakingly made by women in their own homes and sold directly to craft and other tourist-oriented shops.

The number of tourists who visit the islands of Malta each year is three times the size of the country's population.

An aerial view of the harbor and bays in Valletta.

THE DOCKS

The country's dock corporation is mainly owned by the government (61 percent), but Libya has a 30 percent share and Algeria owns 9 percent. The corporation employs thousands of workers to build and repair ships. The origins of this industry go back to the years of imperial rule when Britain's navy and commercial interests required a docking base in the middle of the Mediterranean. When the British pulled out of Malta in the 1970s, the economic implications for the country were grave since many people were employed on the docks. The country, however, has made good use of this asset and has developed its commercial possibilities considerably. Nevertheless, substantial government subsidies are still required.

Malta has also developed the large harbor area around Marsaxlokk, on the eastern side of the island, into an international distribution center for shipping and business. Special storage facilities are available for the blending and storing of oil products and vast warehouses have been constructed for holding shipments of all sizes. The Malta Freeport Terminal, at Marsaxlokk, has developed into a major container terminal in the Mediterranean, equipped with the latest in technology and serving many of the giant operators in the container carrier sector.

Most of Malta's fish supplies are caught by fishermen coming from the Malta Freeport Terminal in Marsaxlokk. Swordfish, tuna, and the popular *lampuka* are caught in abundance between spring and late fall.

TRADE

Malta's main exports are machinery, transportation and electronics equipment, and manufactured and semi-manufactured goods. Principal imports include machinery and transportation equipment, manufactured and semi-manufactured goods, and food, drink, and tobacco. Germany, Italy, Britain, France, and Singapore are Malta's major trading partners. Libya is an important source of energy and mineral fuel. In 2008 Malta's total exports were worth some $3.06 billion, while total imports were valued at about $4.832 billion.

Malta Freeport at Marsaxlokk Bay, with container ships being unloaded by dock cranes.

ENVIRONMENT

A view of the natural bridge and boat at Blue Grotto in Malta.

M

ALTA'S MOST SIGNIFICANT environmental challenges include an inadequate water supply, deforestation, and the preservation of wildlife. The country's extremely limited freshwater resources have led to increasing dependence on desalination.

The nation's agriculture suffers from lack of adequate water for crops due to limited rainfall. Currently 31 percent of Malta's land area is arable and 3 percent is planted with permanent crops.

Rows of terraced farmland in the countryside close to Valletta.

According to United Nations reports, a significant proportion of Malta's animal and plant life is in danger of extinction. Endangered species include the slender-billed curlew, hawksbill turtle, and Atlantic ridley sea turtle. The Mediterranean monk seal, which was sighted sporadically in Malta since 1642, is now no longer in existence in Malta.

A cement factory in Malta. Factories such as these are the main cause of air pollution in the country.

Malta was one of the first countries to ratify the 1976 Barcelona Convention designed to protect the Mediterranean Sea from pollution. Malta's government has made efforts to control environmental damage, including passage of the Environmental Protection Act of 1991 and the creation of a Ministry for the Environment. The Ministry of Health and Environment belongs to the International Union for the Conservation of Nature and Natural Resources. In cooperation with the World Wildlife Fund, the Ghadira wetland area was made a permanent nature reserve in 1980.

CAUSES OF POLLUTION

Malta has no large-scale chemical industry. The major sources of pollution are the power stations, sewage outflows, motor vehicles, and the construction industry. The power stations at Marsa and Delimara, which have both been oil-fired since 1995, emit sulfur dioxide. This chemical is the single most important contributor to acid rain. Acid rain damages buildings, crops, birds, fish, and trees in Malta. Sulfur dioxide also impairs respiration and can trigger asthma attacks.

Cars are the largest source of air pollution in Malta. At present there are more than 266,000 vehicles on the road, and the number is steadily increasing. Many of these vehicles do not use lead-free gasoline. Personal motor vehicles are an extremely unecological means of transportation, and no effort has been made to curb their use. The government has failed to improve a highly inadequate public transport system and the demand for motor cars remains high in a country where the average car trip is around 6.2 miles (10 km) long and 75 percent of dwellings are located within a five-minute walk of a bus stop.

According to a report by Swedish scientists, the Maltese have the second-highest level of lead in the blood of various countries tested worldwide. Although the report did not conclusively indicate the reason for this phenomenon, it showed that the large numbers of cars on the road and the burning of oil and (lead) painted wood in the bakeries are probable causes.

Tap water in Malta is generally of poor quality. There are frequent episodes of high sediment content as well as bouts of sewage contamination after heavy rains.

The Mediterranean Sea, once thought of as one of the cleanest bodies of water in the world, is now one of the most polluted. According to the environmental organization Greenpeace, 1,968,413 tons (2 million metric tons) of crude oil are spilled into the Mediterranean every year. This constitutes one-third of the oil dumped at sea worldwide.

A used car dump in Malta.

Garbage being dumped into the bays and seas of Malta.

Pollution in Malta from industry, housing, and holiday resorts is affecting seabirds in Malta, particularly the Cory's shearwater and European storm-petrel. Pollution in Malta also means wasted energy, which is contributing to global warming, as all of Malta's electricity is produced from hydrocarbons. Given Malta's high population density, noise pollution is also starting to have an effect on many Maltese people's health and quality of life. The Maltese government is lagging behind EU standards, especially when it comes to air pollution, and the Malta Transport Authority, Environment Authority, and Health Department have been accused of ignoring the scientifically proven fact that the health of people—especially children—continues to be jeopardized by blatant pollution from buses (including many private company buses) and many other diesel-powered vehicles. The Maltese government is currently requesting exemption from EU rules on air quality and traffic pollution until mid-2011, but environmental groups in Malta see this as irresponsible, dodging the issue and jeopardizing the population's health. The extensive use of fossil fuels in Malta for transportation, production, and electricity generation is causing health risks for the Maltese population, including lung cancer and heart disease, and the prevalence of asthma among Maltese children and young adults has steadily increased in recent years.

WASTE TREATMENT AND DISPOSAL

WasteServ Malta Ltd. was established in November 2002. The company is responsible for organizing, managing, and operating integrated systems for waste management, including integrated systems for minimization, collection,

Plastic pails being recycled in a facility in Malta.

transportation, sorting, reuse, utilization, recycling, treatment, and disposal of solid and hazardous waste. The company has also launched a number of initiatives, such as the Battery Buster Campaign, where consumers are encouraged to dispose of their used batteries in an environmentally sustainable manner, while at the same time participating in a competition with attractive prizes to be won. The company has also taken over the Regenerative Thermal Oxidizer (RTO) gas compound at the Maghtab Environmental Complex. To date 37,232 tons (37,830 metric tons) of polluting agents has been saved from being released into the atmosphere by the plant.

RECYCLING

WasteServ has implemented a European Union—funded project designed to create training opportunities in small-scale recycling for socially vulnerable groups. The total cost of the project was 150,000 euros, of which the EU co-financed 75 percent. This training program provided a number of selected participants with training in various activities, such as the refurbishment of old furniture and other bulky items, as well as the creation of crafts from material that has been discarded. A spectrum of individuals, including the homeless, people with mental health problems, and ex-offenders, still benefits from this project, since the project is ongoing and is presently being financed through local funds.

CONSERVATION ORGANIZATIONS

Heritage Malta is the national agency for museums, conservation practice, and cultural heritage. Created by the Cultural Heritage Act, which was enacted in 2002, the national agency replaced the former Museums Department. Originally Heritage Malta was entrusted with the management of museums, sites, and their collections, but in 2005, the agency was also charged with the takeover of the former Malta Center for Restoration to become the national agency responsible for conservation. The agency also has a specific educational section with special educational programs targeting children of different age groups as part of organized school visits. These educational programs are based on the educational curriculum and address specific areas of study in an "edutainment" way. The agency also operates the Institute of Conservation and Management of Cultural Heritage, which runs undergraduate and postgraduate academic courses in the field of conservation together with the University of Malta. The Institute also offers a number of short courses to the general public.

Bird Life Malta is the most effective and successful organization in the fight against the illegal hunting of protected bird species in Malta. It organizes an annual Raptor Camp in the fall and Spring Watch Camp in the spring, where participants perform illegal hunting surveillance and monitor raptor

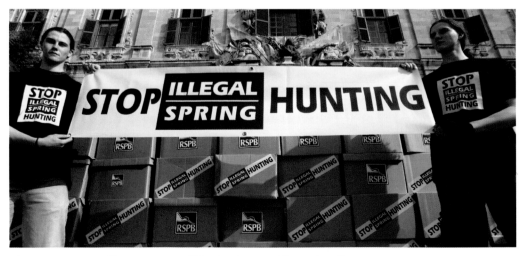

Maltese conservation groups petitioning to stop illegal hunting.

migration. Camp attendees work as "lookout posts," passing on information to the police regarding illegal hunting activities. The volunteers record data on illegal activities and also gather evidence through cameras and video cameras—photographic evidence is proving increasingly important in convicting poachers in Malta, and thanks to evidence collected in Raptor and Spring Watch Camps, Bird Life Malta has had several successful prosecutions in the courts. The mere presence of bird-watchers who will report infringements to the police is an active deterrent to poachers. In 2008 Bird Life Malta's efforts paid off when spring hunting season was not opened in Malta for the first time ever.

The beautiful Maltese rock centaury is the national flower of Malta.

PLANT AND ANIMAL LIFE

The Maltese islands, although small in area (122 square miles/316 square km), host a large number of endemic species, some of which are unique and unusual. These endemic species are important to the Maltese islands because they form part of Maltese national heritage and are topics of scientific research.

FLORA

Although small compared with other countries, the Maltese islands contain many special flowers found only in Malta.

The Maltese rock centaury is the national plant of Malta. The plant is native to the Maltese islands. It is commonly found in the limits of Wied Babu in Malta.

The Maltese everlasting is a species of flowering plant native to Malta. It is a rare endemic bush growing up to 3.3 feet (one metric meter) and found only on the western cliffs of Gozo and on Fungus Rock. Its bright yellow flowers can be seen during the months of May and June. Its long and narrow whitish leaves have a covering of short hair. Its natural habitats are Mediterranean-type shrubby vegetation and rocky shores. It is threatened by habitat loss.

The Maltese pyramidal orchid is a scarce endemic orchid that resembles the common pyramidal orchid, but has smaller and paler pink or white flowers. Its flowers bloom from February to April.

FAUNA

There are more endemic animals than plants in the Maltese islands. Very often, these endemic Maltese animals have been confused with a similar but different species from a neighboring country.

The Maltese freshwater crab.

Bird Life Malta volunteers have increasingly been subject to vandalism of their property, such as cars and observation posts, and verbal abuse. Some volunteers have even had their cars burned and a Bird Life Malta nature reserve has had some trees uprooted.

MALTESE FRESHWATER CRAB The Maltese freshwater crab is endemic to certain areas within the Maltese islands. This subspecies of crab is very rare and its numbers have been decreasing in recent years. The Maltese freshwater crab (known as the *qabru* in Maltese) is a decapod (a crustacean with 10 legs). It can grow up to 3.1 inches (8 cm) in width. It is greenish-gray, with some orange-yellow patches occasionally. The Maltese freshwater crab is found where fresh water or running water is present throughout the year, although it also lives near pools and springs. It is found in Imtahleb, Bahrija, and San Martin in Malta and in Lunzjata Valley in Gozo.

Sadly the numbers of this freshwater crab are steadily declining as a result of the pollution of water, the drying up of streams, and because of the crab's capture by humans.

MALTESE PALPIGRADE The Maltese Palpigrade, endemic to the Maltese islands, comes from a rather primitive order of arachnids. There are 80 species of palpigrade worldwide. They are small and eyeless with a long tail-like structure. The Maltese Palpigrade was first discovered in 1988 when a specimen was found in a cave at Girgenti in Malta. Since then no news of another specimen has been found, making the Maltese Palpigrade a very rare species. The Maltese Palpigrade is 0.05 inches (1.2 millimeters) long and is light brown in color.

MALTESE WALL LIZARD The Filfola lizard or Maltese wall lizard is found in Italy and Malta. This lizard's natural habitats include the Mediterranean-type shrubby vegetation, rocky areas, rocky shores, arable land, pastureland, and rural gardens. In the Maltese islands, there are four subspecies of the Maltese wall lizard. All four subspecies are endemic to the Maltese islands. Unlike the males, which are bright in color, young lizards and females are somewhat dull (brownish).

The Ghadira Nature Reserve of Malta.

NATIONAL PARKS AND RESERVES

GHADIRA NATURE RESERVE The Ghadira Nature Reserve occupies an area of about 14.8 acres (6 hectares) and occupies the floodplain between two ridges. It is some 328 feet (100 m) from Mellieha Bay's sandy beach. More than 200 species of birds have been spotted at the reserve and many birds spend the winter here.

MAJJISTRAL NATURE AND HISTORY PARK The Majjistral Park is situated in the middle of a protected national park, in an area largely dominated by clay, which sits beneath the upper and lower coralline limestone. The wave action has eroded the clay to the point where large sections of limestone have collapsed, forming the boulder scree. This has given rise to a special habitat for flora, which has often remained somewhat protected owing to its relative inaccessibility and a breathtaking landscape. The erosion of the rock has also lead to the formation of sand that in turn is washed ashore to create sandy beaches. The northwest in fact boasts a number of beautiful bays, stretching from Fomm ir-Rih, to Jnejna, Ghajn Tuffieha, Golden Sands, and Paradise Bay. These are all surrounded by magnificent views of clay slopes, boulder scree, and cliffs.

The outstanding landscape in the park has attracted a number of ramblers over the years. While visitors flock to beaches such as Golden Sands in the hot months in order to cool down, the months between October and April bring the landscape to life with the onset of the fall rains. The climate is mild and perfect for walks in the park.

Various features of cultural interest that merit conservation lie within the boundaries of the park. These features include cart-ruts, long rubble walls (dry stone walls), farmhouses, small beehives, tombs dating to the Classical period, natural caves, and numerous stone huts that lie within and outside the park. Of particular interest is a rare stone hut constructed in a square shape. Rural stone huts were used for both storage and shelter.

On the two sides of the valley overlooking Golden Bay (ir-Ramla tal-Mixquqa), there are entrenchments built as part of a coastal defense system during the period of the Knights of Saint John, in the early 18th century.

Il Majjistral Park is the first national park to be set up in Malta.

Filfla is a small, barren, uninhabited islet located 3.1 miles (5 km) south of Malta, and is the most southerly point of the Maltese archipelago. There is a small rocky islet next to Filfla, called Filfoletta.

Filfla has an area of just 15 acres (6 ha). It is a crumbling flat-topped limestone plateau surrounded by 197-foot-high (60-m-high) cliffs. The only known permanent structure on it was a chapel built inside a cave in 1343, which was destroyed by an earthquake in 1856 that also sank part of the island. Until 1971 the Royal Navy and Royal Air Force used the island for target practice. It became a bird reserve in 1980. Three species of sea birds breed on the islet: the European storm petrel, Cory's shearwater, and yellow-legged gull. A type of wall lizard and a kind of door snail are endemic to Filfla. A large wild leek, growing up to 6.6 feet (2 m) high, also grows here.

The Filfla Natural Reserve Act, enacted in 1988, provided for further restrictions on access and use, including a prohibition on fishing within a nautical mile (1.9 km) around the island due to the possibility of encountering unexploded ordnance. Access to Filfla is only possible for educational or scientific purposes, and visitors must get prior permission from the Ministry responsible for the environment.

On the Maltese coast opposite Filfla are the archaeological sites of Hagar Qim and Mnajdra and a memorial to Walter Norris Congreve, one of Malta's British governors-general, who was buried at sea in the channel between the island and Malta.

THE MALTESE

Maltese men in medieval costume at Fort Saint Elmo.

MALTA IS NOT A multiethnic society and the Maltese are a remarkably homogeneous people. This helps explain the strong sense of national pride that binds the people together. However, as its long history makes clear, the country has been conquered and ruled by a series of more powerful nations, and Malta has only been an independent nation since 1964.

Local children posing for a shot. The Maltese people have often been described by others as gregarious and friendly.

It is not surprising, therefore, that facial features reveal a mix of influences. Although the Maltese are a highly individual race, the face of a Maltese reflects a fairly unique fusion of the West (through the rule of ancient Rome and later European powers) and an Arab influence that goes back to the days of the Phoenicians.

CHARACTERISTICS

Because the Maltese have been exposed for so long to other cultural influences, many national characteristics are the result of a blending of foreign cultures. To a lesser or greater degree, this is true of nearly all cultures, but it applies particularly to the Maltese. A good example is the very strong attachment to the Roman Catholic faith and its practices that is also found in Italy and especially Sicily, which is closer to Malta than to the Italian mainland.

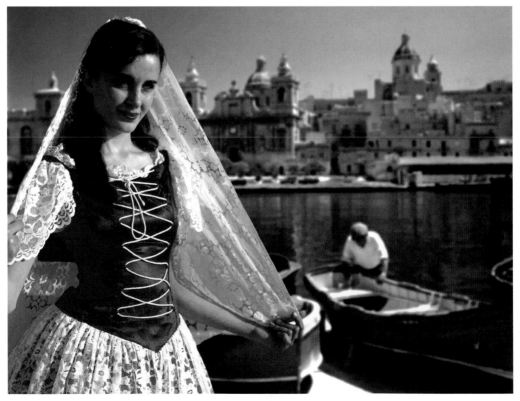

A girl dressed in the traditional clothes of Malta.

Crowds of people walking along Republic Street in Valletta.

An important difference, and one that goes some way to explaining what is unique about the Maltese, is Malta's internationalism. The country has been, and because of mass tourism, continues to be remarkably open to foreign influences.

Yet, despite this, the people maintain their own dignity and way of life without feeling threatened or aggrieved in any way. The "no little kindness" that the Bible records as being afforded to Saint Paul is an aspect of Maltese hospitality, which many tourists feel is a distinguishing and highly attractive aspect of the culture. Many foreign tourists enjoy coming to the country because they feel they are treated with the same respect that the Maltese extend to their own people.

Many Maltese have a strong, almost old-fashioned, sense of dignity and manners. This is partly because Malta is not subjected to the relentless pace of modern European society. The more relaxed lifestyle allows people to interact with others in a way that seems almost stress-free.

POPULATION

The current population of Malta is 405,165, including about 31,000 people on Gozo. This makes the country one of the world's more heavily populated areas. This is especially true of the main island of Malta, where about half the total population lives in a small urban area around Valletta and the Grand Harbour. One reason for this comparatively large population is because the Church has been able to discourage the use of contraception and, until recently at least, families tended to be large.

The old Maltese attitude in which Gozitans were stereotyped as "uneducated" and "primitive" is now changing, as more Gozitans move to Malta to seek higher education and better economic opportunities.

About 115,973 Maltese live overseas, mostly in Australia and Canada. The population of Malta also undergoes a massive, although temporary, surge every summer when 1.2 million tourists fly in to enjoy the hospitable climate, the beaches, and the welcoming atmosphere. About half a million summer visitors come from Britain.

The British also make up the majority of the 6,500 foreign residents who live on the islands. Many of them are senior citizens who have chosen to retire in Malta.

GOZITANS

About 31,000 people live on the island of Gozo, and although they are Maltese, they always refer to themselves as "Gozitans." This is more an expression of their sense of pride than a wish to be independent of Malta. The people of Gozo have a sense of their own identity as islanders, but they have no serious political disagreement with the Maltese government, nor do they have any wish to be treated as a separate group. There are, however, some noticeable differences in outlook between the people who live on the island of Malta and those who have lived all their lives on Gozo. Gozitans are more accustomed to a rural way of life and, up until very recently, they have not benefited as much from economic progress.

A group of elderly local women in Malta.

Edward De Bono, one of the world's most famous psychologists, is renowned for his popular books on ways of educating the mind to think more creatively. The phrase lateral thinking, *as opposed to conventional ways of thinking that seek to categorize knowledge in an unimaginative manner, is often associated with De Bono.*

Many people consider De Bono a pioneer in the field of psychology and someone whose ideas have had important implications for methods of teaching and learning. De Bono was born in Malta in 1933 and studied medicine there before going to England, where he also studied psychology.

NICKNAMES

Nicknames, as a familiar way of identifying certain people, are common to many cultures around the world, but in Malta they are woven into the fabric of everyday life. In rural communities they still play a part in social life. According to sociologists the relatively limited number of surnames available in Malta accounts for the common practice of identifying individuals by nicknames. One village, consisting of nearly 250 different households, was found to have fewer than 60 surnames, so the use of nicknames serves a practical purpose.

What is interesting about nicknames in Malta is that they can be used as a familiar term of address. This is fairly unique to Malta. In neighboring Mediterranean cultures, such as Sicily, for example, many nicknames are insults and would never be used to actually address a person. Maltese nicknames, on the other hand, are mainly harmless. For example, a man whose hobby is catching birds with a homemade trap may be known by the name of a particular species of bird.

LIFESTYLE

A shopkeeper sitting outside his shop in Malta.

AN UNHURRIED PACE IS A CENTRAL characteristic of Maltese life and it is reflected in the people's lifestyle in various ways. The Maltese work hard, but not to the extreme. They enjoy good conversation and exchanging news, and many festive events bear testimony to their capacity to enjoy life outside of work.

The Maltese lifestyle could very generally be described as a Mediterranean one, but there are individual inflections that are uniquely Maltese.

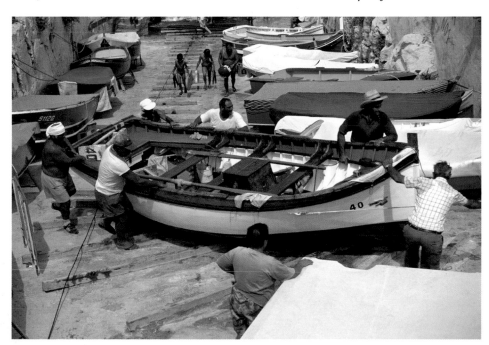

Fishermen preparing to bring their boats to sea in the morning.

A mobile fruit vendor in the fishing village of Marsaskala. A visit to the local market is an essential part of the week's activities for many families.

THE WORKING DAY

Most working Maltese tend to rise early. Farmers and other outdoor workers often start work around 7:00 A.M. Office workers and employees in manufacturing plants and factories usually start work an hour later, or by 9:00 A.M. at the latest. By this time shops are generally open.

Small bakeries and butchers open early in the morning and vendors selling fresh vegetables set up in their regular locations by erecting a small table extension from the back of their small vans. Many shops close for a few hours during the hottest part of the afternoon. This afternoon rest period, the siesta, is common to most Mediterranean cultures. Nevertheless some visitors may find it strange that so many places close and then spring back to life in the late afternoon, when shops remain open until about 7:00 P.M.

The relaxed pace of the Maltese lifestyle is typified by the absence of the modern supermarket that is so common in other parts of Western Europe and in North America. In Malta people have time to shop, and they do not expect—or, in many cases, even wish—to find everything on their shopping list under one roof. Fresh meat, bread, and vegetables are still mostly bought from small vendors, who draw their customers from particular areas.

STREET MARKETS

Virtually every town and village in Malta has a designated market area, although it may be tucked away in a side street or situated in one of the quieter corners of the town. If a visitor turned up after midday, there would be nothing to see or buy, because most of the vendors would have packed up and shoppers gone home by 11:00 A.M. In some of the larger towns, a street is blocked off to traffic on market day as vendors turn up in their vans and set up their tables according to a strict pattern. Fresh produce such as vegetables and fish are at one end of the street, while clothes and household items usually dominate the opposite end of the street or the other side of the square.

Markets in Malta always draw a big crowd.

Many of the items that in would be bought in a supermarket or specialty store in other parts of Europe or North America are readily available on market day in Maltese towns and villages. Aside from various types of food and the staples that are always bought, market day is the occasion for buying clothing, household goods ranging from can-openers to small carpets, as well as decorative figures for display in the home.

Some items have prices marked, but most do not and some friendly bargaining is common. Malta's biggest market takes place every Sunday morning outside the walls of Valletta, near the main bus terminal. There is also a food market inside Valletta on weekdays. Market days in Malta also fulfill an important social role—local residents can meet their neighbors and friends in an informal setting and exchange news and gossip.

HOMES

The people of Malta enjoy a modest and quiet lifestyle, characterized by a self-contentment that is reflected in the typical Maltese home. From the outside, there is often little to distinguish one home from another, and very few people go out of their way to assert individuality or extravagant wealth.

Modern houses like these are also found in Malta.

Typical homes in a Maltese town.

The common use of large blocks of pale-colored limestone as building material for construction helps contribute to this apparent uniformity.

The high temperatures that characterize the long summer months have influenced the choice of building materials inside the house. Most modern homes have floors made of smooth marble or ceramic tiles because they do not retain heat.

There is a common sense of pride in keeping the interior spotlessly clean. Invariably a room is set aside as the "best room," a sitting room that is reserved for receiving guests. It is here where a family asserts its social identity. The best furniture is placed in this room and framed photographs of the family are hung from the walls or perhaps placed on a cabinet that contains drinks for the social occasions that bring guests into the house.

A reasonably well-to-do home usually has certain items of furniture and decoration. Crystal chandeliers, often of the highly ornate kind, are very popular, as is handmade wooden furniture. A special chest or cabinet will be regularly polished so that it gleams as if new.

THE FARMING LIFE

The typical farm is small and family-run. Malta's rocky terrain and generally poor soil does not support large-scale farming, and there are few large commercial farms dedicated to a single crop. Many farms, especially on Gozo, which has some reasonably good agricultural land, grow a surprisingly rich variety of vegetables. Potatoes, onions, tomatoes, cabbage, lettuce, and cauliflower are grown throughout the year. Malta's warm temperatures also allow eggplant, pumpkins, figs, oranges, and lemons to be grown.

In addition the hospitable climate allows for up to four crops of potatoes to be planted in the same year, so a small farmer can keep busy throughout the year. Much of the farmer's produce goes to the weekly markets in local villages and towns. Some farmers park their vans on a street corner and display baskets and cases of their produce.

Local farmers harvesting their zucchini plants.

The Maltese lifestyle can generally be described as relaxed and laidback when compared to that in other European countries and in North America, but even Malta island seems hectic compared to the small neighboring island of Gozo. It was only recently that the first two sets of traffic lights were installed on the island, and the volume of traffic is still remarkably light. The main roads are lined with white and red oleander, and the absence of industry and factories gives the island an atmosphere of tranquility.

Gozo has 13 villages but 22 churches, indicating the pervasive role of religion in the islanders' lifestyle. Summer festivals are marked by fireworks and marching bands, but the religious basis of these celebrations is strongly felt by most Gozitans.

The extended family is still the norm on the island, and a home shared by two or three generations is common. Rural values of thrift and conservatism are deeply rooted among Gozitans.

On Gozo there are still traditional farms that have changed little in the last 50 years. A television antenna or satellite dish may be attached to the exterior of the house, but the design of the house and the lifestyle of its inhabitants are still rooted in a rural tradition of self-sufficiency and hard work. Farm houses may be over 100 years old, and although they are equipped with modern household appliances, the architecture remains more Arab than European. Houses tend to be flat-roofed, small, and square, and built of honey-colored stone that merges with the natural colors of the landscape. The floors are also built with blocks of stone that are kept clean and cool by regular oiling and polishing.

EDUCATION

School attendance is compulsory from the ages of 5 to 16 and is free in government schools and institutions, from kindergarten to college. Kindergarten classes cater to 3- and 4-year-olds. Children attend elementary school until the age of 11, then move on to secondary education. Some students go to a trade school or craft center after three years of secondary education, where they pursue less academic, more practical subjects. Others take examinations at the age of 16.

Every year well over half of students who reach the age of 16 choose to continue their education. A variety of post-secondary courses is available, ranging from academic programs designed as pre-university courses to vocational programs in areas such as tourism, agriculture, health care, and technical education. The University of Malta, which has more than 9,000 Maltese students at any given time, also attracts more than 700 foreign or exchange students from nearly 80 different countries.

The Catholic Church still plays an important role in education, and runs its own schools alongside state schools. Under an agreement between the Church and the state of Malta, Catholic schools are free of charge. About 30 percent of all students attend the non-state (both Catholic and private) schools.

The University of Malta is the oldest university in the British Commonwealth outside of Britain. The university's history dates back to 1592, when the Jesuits founded the college, which became renowned for its scholarship throughout the Mediterranean. In 1768 it became a university.

POLITICS

Politics is woven into the fabric of Maltese life in a way that is quite different from in the United States. Although the situation is changing, especially among the younger generation of Maltese, there is still much truth to the notion that a Maltese is born into a political party. Family loyalties are often closely tied to one of the two main parties, and this works at a very basic level. It is not unknown for a family to prefer to shop at a particular place, or even more strongly wish to avoid a particular shop, because of the proprietor's political beliefs.

BUS TRAVEL

Buses in Malta, besides being a means of transportation, are very much a part of the Maltese lifestyle. Although many people own cars, public transportation still plays an important role in many people's lives. This is especially true for older citizens and young people who do not have their own cars.

Since a 7-mile (11-km) stretch of railway was closed in 1931, the bus network has been the sole means of public transportation and has spread to encompass nearly every corner of the main island.

No village on the island of Malta is more than an hour's trip by bus to the capital.

Passengers boarding a bus in Malta.

Malta's classic buses have become tourist attractions in their own right, due to their uniqueness, and are depicted on many Maltese advertisements to promote tourism as well as on gifts and merchandise for tourists. The buses in Malta are all dark yellow, with a band of orange, while those on the sister island of Gozo are gray, with a red band.

The hub of the bus network, and the place from which nearly all the island's buses operate, is a large square and roundabout immediately outside the walls of Valletta. From about 6:00 A.M. until around 11:00 P.M., this area bustles with activity as a constant stream of buses moves in and out. Although Malta has some modern air-conditioned vehicles, decades-old buses are more common. The way their exteriors are decorated with various stickers and metal emblems gives the buses individuality. It is not uncommon to find a nickname or pet name for the bus written across the hood. Malta buses carry approximately 31 million passengers per year.

Cars more than 20 years old are commonplace on Malta's roads.

VEHICLE WORSHIP

There is about one car for every two adults in Malta, and very few families do not own a vehicle. Because not everyone can afford a new car, few cars are scrapped. Most Maltese, at one time or another, deal with the second-hand car market, and older cars that would rapidly lose their value in other parts of Europe keep their value for a lot longer in Malta. Small auto repair businesses are common, and many Maltese take great pride in keeping a car that is no longer manufactured in running condition. Car ownership in Malta is the fourth-highest in the European Union—1,508 automobiles per square mile (582 automobiles per square km).

A traditional form of transportation, dating back to the mid-19th century, is the horse-drawn carriage known as karozzin (ca-rotts-SEEN). These vehicles hold up to four passengers on high seats, with a canopy to provide shade. They are still used by some Maltese, especially on Gozo, for short trips, such as a social visit to friends on a Sunday. They are currently more of a tourist attraction than anything else.

It is this tradition of looking after old cars that helps explain the regard that many people have toward vehicles. Owners like to decorate their cars with stickers and emblems, while trucks and public buses get special treatment. The driver's area of a public bus may even be transformed into a mini-shrine, with small plastic statues, religious pictures and icons, and dried flowers in glass vases.

RELIGION

A beautiful gothic-styled church in Malta.

MALTA IS STRONGLY AND predominantly Roman Catholic, yet its Catholicism has qualities unlike those of other Catholic countries. This is evident in the multitude of festivals that take place every year, for although they nearly all have a religious origin, they are regarded by many Maltese as festive, social events.

While the Maltese islands were under the dominion of the Knights of Malta, from the 15th century through to the late 18th century, the grand master had the status of a prince of the Catholic Church, and enjoyed a special relationship with the Pope, which occasionally led to a considerable amount of friction with the local bishops.

The ornate interior of Saint Paul's Cathedral in Malta.

Like many other European countries, Malta has changed with the times. The Roman Catholic Church no longer wields the enormous power it once had over people's daily lives. Besides Catholicism, there are several other religious groups in Malta, including Anglicans, Methodists, Greek Orthodox, Jews, Muslims, and some small evangelical groups. Under the country's constitution, Roman Catholicism is the state religion and must be taught in state schools.

CHRISTIANITY

According to legend, Christianity came to Malta with one of Christ's disciples, Saint Paul, who was shipwrecked on the island. At the time, Malta was occupied by the Romans and Saint Paul was brought to the capital and allowed to preach Christianity. The Roman governor, Publius, and his family were converted and he ordered that Christianity become the religion of the country. In this way Malta became one of the first countries in the world to adopt Christianity.

The shipwreck of Saint Paul off the coast of Malta. The Maltese believe this event led to the introduction of Christianity on the island.

Malta is the only country in Europe that does not permit divorce.

The period of Arab domination interrupted Christian rule, but it was resumed with the arrival of the Normans, who reestablished the religion on an official basis. In 1530 the Knights of the Order of Saint John arrived on the island, giving a new impetus to the hold of the religion over the people. After a very short period of anticlerical French rule under Napoleon, the Church reestablished its power during the 19th and 20th centuries.

Under British rule, the missionary activities of other churches were restricted, and in 1922 the Roman Catholic religion was recognized in law as the religion of the country. A section of the Malta Criminal Code was passed, making it a criminal offense to criticize the Catholic religion in public. It is this long, uninterrupted, and unchallenged period of Catholic influence that is still felt today in Malta.

HOW TO UPSET EVERYONE IN EIGHT DAYS

Napoleon brought 700 years of Christian rule in Malta to an abrupt end when the French drove the Knights from the islands in 1798. Napoleon himself only remained in Malta for eight days, but in that time he tried to make too many changes too quickly and stirred up popular discontent as a result.

Some of the changes he instituted were well received, such as establishing a council of Maltese to administer the islands and creating government schools, but his attacks on the power of the Church misfired. He set up civil marriages so that people could marry outside of a church, limited the power of Malta's bishop to purely Church affairs, and abolished the practice in which members of the clergy could charge fees for their services. To make matters worse, the French did not have enough money to ensure that the changes were made smoothly, so they attempted to auction off the property of a church in Mdina. Led by influential Christians, the people rose in rebellion and the main French force had to take refuge in Valletta.

A Maltese man making his confession to a priest.

According to tradition, there are no poisonous snakes in Malta because Saint Paul removed all their venom after being bitten by one soon after he arrived.

As late as the 1950s the Church dominated social life and determined the educational and social activities of the young in ways that are no longer acceptable in Western countries. The Church ran its own schools, paid no taxes, and owned large tracts of land and property on the islands. Priests could not be prosecuted under Maltese law. The disputes of the 1950s and 1960s with the Labour Party postponed the inevitable decline of Church power but could not prevent it. Today religion in Malta is no longer a matter of social pressure but one of choice.

The islands of Malta form an archdiocese, with an archbishop based in Valletta and two cathedrals. Gozo has its own bishop. The islands have 359 churches, many of them medieval in origin, and there are about a thousand priests. Fifty-six homes for Christian brothers and 103 convents are also found on the islands.

ROMAN CATHOLICISM

Roman Catholicism emphasizes the role of the Virgin Mary. Small grottoes dedicated to the mother of Jesus Christ are maintained throughout the island. Another way in which the Roman Catholic Church differs from other forms of Christianity is in the role of the head of the Church, the Pope. His decisions are considered infallible, which means that the various policies that are issued by the Vatican must be followed by all Catholics. On a tiny island like Malta, which has had a serious problem with overpopulation for some time, the Church's restriction on birth control has caused much soul-searching. This issue was part of the battle that took place between the Church and the Labour Party in the 1950s and 1960s.

SAINT PAUL

Originally a Jew from Asia Minor, Saint Paul was born in A.D. 6 and trained as a rabbi. In his early years he actively persecuted Christians, believing them to be a breakaway Jewish sect, but on a journey to Damascus one day he had a vision of Christ telling him to become a missionary for Christianity. His life thereafter was a series of missionary journeys across Greece and as far as Malta, where he was shipwrecked en route to Rome.

The Church of Saint Paul in Rabat is said to be the first parish church on the islands. Near it is a grotto where the saint is believed to have spent most of his time while on Malta. The walls of the grotto are believed to have miraculous curative properties. Beneath the church are catacombs built into the soft limestone rock where tables have been carved into the rock for people to celebrate Christ's last supper. On his return from Malta, Saint Paul was arrested after riots by Jewish groups against his preaching and was executed in Rome in A.D. 62.

OTHER RELIGIONS

Most congregants at the local Protestant churches are not Maltese; many retired British people live in the country, and vacationers from many other nations compose the remainder of such congregations. In 2008 the seven congregations of Jehovah's Witnesses reported 569 active members, with an annual attendance of 1,120. There is one Greek Catholic church, which also hosts Russian Orthodox services a few times a year (when a patriarch comes over from Moscow to celebrate Mass for the Eastern Orthodox holidays, like Easter). There is one Muslim mosque and one Jewish congregation. Zen Buddhism and the Bahá'í Faith also have about 40 members. There is one Muslim mosque and a Muslim primary school. Of the estimated 3,000 Muslims in Malta, approximately 2,250 are foreigners, approximately 600 are naturalized citizens, and approximately 150 are native-born Maltese.

A shrine in Valletta—one of many found around Malta.

PRACTICE AND SUPERSTITIONS

Most Maltese have a personal saint to whom they appeal in times of need. Many churches hold collections of votive paintings dedicated to a particular saint after an intercession or a cure, as well as other items dedicated to the saint, such as crutches no longer needed after a miracle cure. Shrines dot the island—in small grottoes, in offices and shops, and even in buses. As in many other Catholic countries people make the sign of the cross as they pass a church and stand still at the midday and evening Angelus when the church bells are rung.

For most people in Malta, there is a point where religious belief mixes with superstition. For example, the design of some baroque churches on the island is part superstition and part practicality. These churches have two towers and one tower always contains a clock, which in the olden days was the only clock in the whole village. To keep the symmetry of the church front, another clock was put on the other tower. Since a real clock was too expensive and unnecessary, a clock face was often painted on the tower. The time on the painted clock face always shows a few minutes before midnight, the witching hour. At midnight the devil is said to roam, looking for souls. Seeing the hands of the clock at 11:55 P.M. confuses the devil and prevents him from carrying out his evil work.

There are many other signs of superstition in Malta. Women wear coral necklaces to ward off evil, while many rural houses have a pair of bull's horns tied high up on a corner of the house. A niche around the house may also hold a figure of a saint. Another example of superstition on the islands are the *luzzijiet* ("LUT-tsie-yiet"), the fishing boats that are always named after a saint and have eyes painted on the stern to keep the boats watchful. The painted eyes, known as the eyes of Osiris, after an ancient Egyptian god, are regarded by the superstitious as a means of warding off evil, but their use today is more as a traditional symbol of good luck.

The Church of Our Lady of Victory in Malta shows the symmetrical bell towers and clocks found in many churches in the country.

This is an ancient Latin phrase that can be translated as "Do not hold this church to be free from the law." It is often seen by the main door of small churches around the island. The phrase dates back to the period before the 19th century, when the Church had sole jurisdiction over all matters within its property, much like modern-day embassies where the laws of the host country do not apply.

Criminals on the run could seek sanctuary in a church. In order to prevent churches from filling up with criminals, the Church authorities put up these signs giving up Church jurisdiction wherever the signs were posted. Churches without the Latin inscription could, however, still be used for sanctuary. In 1828 the British governor proclaimed an end to the sanctuary law.

THE CHRISTIAN CALENDAR

In Malta the major Christian festivals are celebrated in traditional style. A Maltese tradition at Christmas is to give children shallow saucers of water in which are sown wheat seeds or other seeds. The seeds are kept in the dark until they sprout. They are then placed by the family's nativity scene, by the crib of the baby Jesus. This tradition may be a remnant of an earlier religion in which the harvest was significant.

Easter is traditionally celebrated with a procession on Good Friday. Penitents make the journey in as uncomfortable a way as they can. Young men are often hooded and wear white robes with heavy chains on their ankles. The belief is that the farther they can walk in such discomfort, the more of their sins will be forgiven.

An Easter procession in Malta.

Every village has its own patron saint, and the feast day of that saint is always celebrated on the weekend nearest to the actual day. These feast days are very often the day of the year in which they died. Although this was once a religious event, most people today see it as a secular occasion.

CELEBRATING THE PATRON SAINT

Malta's traditional festivals are primarily social occasions today, but they still retain a religious significance based on the worship of a patron saint of a village or town. The pealing of church bells may be drowned out by the sound of exploding fireworks, but for devout Catholics a visit to their church is the most important part of these festivities. Much effort and care goes into decorating the church inside and outside, and the climax of the event is still the procession where a life-sized statue of the patron saint is paraded through the streets.

Three days of prayer precede the festival. Every evening, singing takes place in the church, followed by Mass and a special service known as Benediction. Each village has its own hymn to its patron saint in a popular melody and an anthem set to operatic music. These evening services end with members of the congregation kissing the saint's relic, which is enshrined in an ornately decorated gold case.

The Siggiewi church is lit up by thousands of bulbs during the Saint Nicholas *festa*. Lights and fireworks have become an important part of festivities to celebrate the patron saint.

Sculptures pay tribute to one of Malta's many patrons, Saint Anthony.

On the eve of the feast day, another special service takes place in the church. When Mass is over, a hymn of praise, known as the Te Deum, from the first words of the Latin hymn, is sung. The life-sized statue of the saint rests overnight in the center of the nave and bouquets of flowers are arranged around it as an act of homage. In the evening the holy relic is solemnly carried from a side chapel to the main altar.

On the evening of the feast day itself, the statue of the saint is carried shoulder-high out of the church and through the streets, while the relic of the saint is solemnly carried by a church dignitary. Monks and priests, dressed in their finest vestments, join the procession alongside lay members of devotional associations. These members wear their own colorful robes and walk behind their own huge banner displaying an emblem of their group.

SOME OTHER SAINTS

Each tiny village in Malta has its own saint, as does each profession. Some of the saints have particularly gruesome stories of martyrdom. Saint Agatha, whose chapel is in Mdina, is the patron saint of Malta. She fled to Malta from Italy in A.D. 249, after refusing to marry the governor of Catania at the wish of Emperor Decius. In Malta she was said to have spent her time in catacombs under the city, teaching and praying. When she left Malta and returned to Catania in 251, she was imprisoned and tortured before being burned to death.

Saint Luke is another famous person to have spent time on the island. He accompanied Paul on his journeys. A physician, he is the patron saint of doctors, students, butchers, and artists. Saint Publius converted Malta to Christianity. He was made bishop of Malta and then Athens. Later martyred, he became a saint.

Around the islands at the numerous shrines to the saints are objects known as niccec *(nee-chech), padlocked boxes embedded in the shrine. These are contribution boxes where those in search of intercession from the saint can drop in some money, which goes to the local church or a charity.*

ANCIENT RELIGIONS

The temples at Ggantija are believed to be the oldest freestanding monuments in the world, predating the pyramids. The remains of the temples suggest an Earth-worshiping civilization with complex religious ceremonies. Altars show evidence of animal sacrifice with libations of blood and milk. Priestesses could have stood behind curtains and in hidden chambers in the rock, issuing predictions, and people may have come to the temples to ask the oracles for advice. Burials made around the same time were complex, suggesting also the Earth-mother worship indicated by the temples.

The altars at the Hagar Qim temple offer a glimpse of a vanished religion.

Around 3000 B.C. the community built the Hypogeum, a series of underground burial chambers, at Paola. It was discovered by chance and contained fragments of bone and pottery. The walls were decorated with patterns and symbols and an oracle chamber was cut into the wall. It would have echoed the priest's voice and made it seem more supernatural. At Tarxien, a statue of the Earth goddess has been discovered.

L. PSAILA 212 212
BRITISH CONFECTIONERY

WHOLESALE & RETAIL

SWEET SHOP

LANGUAGE

A British sweet shop in Malta.

M ALTA'S OFFICIAL LANGUAGES are Maltese and English. There are few people in Malta who cannot speak some English, but the Maltese language is alive and well, and it is not an endangered language. Italian is also spoken, or at least understood, by many Maltese. Few citizens are monolingual. Maltese can, however, be difficult to master because of its complex pronunciation rules.

Maltese girls laughing while having a conversation.

Before the arrival of the British, the official language since 1530 had been Italian, but this was downgraded by the increased use of English. In 1934 English and Maltese were declared the sole official languages. At that time only about 15 percent of the population could speak English. This meant that out of 58,000 males qualified by age to be jurors, only 767 could qualify by language, as only Italian had been used in the courts until then.

A Maltese sign to clean up after your dog in Sliema. Although spoken by fewer than a million people around the world, Maltese is a living language that is in no danger of dying out.

MALTESE

The Maltese language reveals the mixed history of the country. There is no evidence of influence by the Phoenician or Roman cultures, but the arrival of the Arabs in the ninth century was to have a profound effect on the language.

The first Maltese dictionaries were compiled in the 17th century, although the earliest prose writing in Maltese that has survived is a collection of religious sermons from 1739. The language of the sermons betrays a strong Italian influence in its choice of vocabulary, which is not surprising given that the Church in Malta at that time was largely made up of Sicilians. It was only in 1934 that Maltese became the official language of the law courts, which until then had used Italian.

Here are some basic everyday expressions that you might like to try using. The first two words show a French influence and are pronounced very much like their French equivalents, while the word for "thank you" reveals the influence of Italian:

The historical source of modern Maltese vocabulary is 52 percent Italian/Sicilian, 32 percent Sicilian-Arabic, and 6 percent English, with some of the remainder being French.

Bongu (BON-joo)	Good morning
Bonswa (BON-swah)	Good evening
Sahha (sah-har)	Good-bye
Jekk joghgbok (ye-hek YOJ-bok)	Please
Grazzi (GRAHT-see)	Thank you
Iva (EE-vah)	Yes
Le (leh)	No

The Maltese language is the only Semitic tongue that is written in the Latin script and the only official Semitic language of the European Union.

ARAB INFLUENCE

At a very basic structural level, Maltese can be regarded as an Arabic dialect. In terms of families of languages Maltese belongs to the Semitic group, the word *Semitic* being used to describe a set of languages that include Arabic and Hebrew. That Maltese remains a Semitic language is quite remarkable, considering that nearly 1,000 years have passed since the Arabs lost control of Malta to the Normans. When the Arabs first arrived, there was, of course, a language already being used by the native population, but this was effectively replaced by the language of the conquerors. Around 10,000 Maltese words are of Semitic origin, but this is not a particularly large percentage of the total vocabulary. There are more words of non-Semitic origin in the Maltese language, but interestingly many of the basic words that belong to the ordinary, everyday world of living are Arabic in origin. This reflects how Arab influence impacted the lives of ordinary people.

An Arabic sign being painted in Malta. Although there are thousands of words of Italian and Sicilian origin in the Maltese language today, the basic structure of the language remains Arabic.

That some Maltese words used to describe Christian ideas are also Arabic in origin suggest that the early Christians who came to Malta continued to use the Arabic language. Curiously, the Maltese word for "father," *missier* (MISS-ir), is a Romance word, while *omm* (OMM), the word for "mother," is Arabic. This might be because the Normans, who first introduced Romance words to Malta, would have intermarried with native, Arabic-speaking women. In this way the two cultures kept their hold on the common language that eventually evolved.

ROMANCE INFLUENCE

Romance languages—the main ones being Italian, French, and Spanish—are languages that developed from the spoken form of Latin used in the Roman Empire. It was the Normans who first brought a new, non-Arabic language to Malta, but although they introduced a large stock of new words from Romance vocabulary, they did not change the fundamental structure of the language, which remained Semitic.

The Norman lords who settled in Malta did not maintain the same degree of contact with the native population as the Arabs. The Maltese learned many new words, but they did not acquire a grammar that could replace the Arabic structure of the language they spoke. The input of Romance words into the Maltese vocabulary continued under the rule of the Spanish kingdoms and the Order of Saint John.

The men who made up the Order of Saint John came from the aristocratic families of Europe, and their linguistic influence was felt in Malta over a period of 250 years. Like the Normans, they did not have much contact with the peasants of the islands. So although new words were constantly being added, the structure of the language spoken by ordinary people remained largely unchanged. The earliest examples of Maltese literature date back to the 17th century.

Elderly Maltese men having a conversation. A large section of the Maltese population is bilingual or even trilingual. Besides Maltese and English, Italian is also understood by many people.

THE ITALIAN CONNECTION

The Maltese constitution was suspended by the British in the early 1930s, mainly as the result of a controversial attempt to promote Italian as the official language. The British claimed that only about 15 percent of the population spoke Italian. Italy's political leader, Benito Mussolini, on the other

SOME TRADITIONAL PROVERBS

- *The word of a Maltese is more reliable than the oath of a king.*
- *A sleeping man catches no fish.*
- *If you cut off the tail of a pig it will always remain a pig.*
- *An agreement between two people is reached in two days; an agreement between three requires two months.*
- *Expect the worst, so that the good may not be lacking.*
- *Money breeds money and worms breed worms.*
- *Mountain does not meet mountain, but a face meets another face.*
- *Enjoy yourself, for there is nothing in the world we can call our own.*
- *There is no rose without thorns.*

hand, claimed that the Maltese language was a dialect of Italian and that the Maltese people were Italian by race. There was, however, no linguistic basis to this claim, and the real nature of Mussolini's interest in Malta became clear when World War II broke out and Italian planes bombed the island.

ENGLISH IN MALTA

English was first introduced to Malta in the early 19th century when the British, then at war with France, took over the islands after the French garrison surrendered. At that time the ruling class in Malta, including government officials and the Church, mostly spoke Italian and little changed for a long time after the arrival of the British. English made little headway in Malta in the 19th century because the British exercised political power but did not mix on a daily basis with ordinary people. In this way they were not very different from the Normans or the Knights of Saint John.

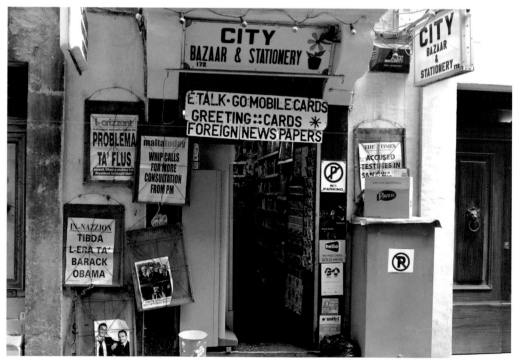

A book and stationery shop in Malta. English-speaking visitors to Malta have little difficulty communicating with the Maltese because of the widespread use of English on the islands.

From the Romance languages

A large part of the Maltese vocabulary is derived from words of Romance origin, especially Sicilian and Italian words. These include the majority of words associated with religious life; words for the months of the year; words used in the house such as "bedroom," "dining room," and kitchen objects; and most words relating to ships, the army, forms of entertainment, and the different trades and professions.

From the Arabic world

The names for certain directions of the wind; the bastions of the city walls; words such as "roof" and "floor;" basic foods, such as bajd *(BITE, eggs); most names of fishes, fruits, trees, plants, and seeds; and basic verbs related to education, such as* qara *(RA, to read),* kiteb *(kee-TEP, to write),* ghadd *(ADD, to count), and* tghallem *(tull-LEMM, to learn).*

It was only in the 20th century that English began to play an increasingly important role in the lives of the Maltese people. The replacement of Italian with English in the education system starting in the 1930s was pivotal because this affected ordinary young people and not just the educated elite. In the 1960s Malta developed as a popular holiday destination for British tourists. An important reason for this, apart from the appealing climate of a Mediterranean island, was the perception that Malta was friendly toward the British. The long history of imperial rule had accustomed the Maltese to the habits of the British, and English was not an unfamiliar language. As tourism became increasingly important to the Maltese economy, and as English established itself as the world's international language, the Maltese became more and more willing to learn and use English.

A street sign in Maltese and English in Mdina.

Malta entered the 21st century as a bilingual society, where English and Maltese are used fluently as the means of communication, both officially and informally.

THE POLITICS OF LANGUAGE

Although English is now widely spoken in Malta, the first attempts to introduce the language into the education system created much resentment among the Maltese upper class. In 1880 a British report recommended that English instead of Italian should be taught in the country's elementary schools and that only English should be used in the university. This was not well received by the country's non-British elite. This small class of educated people, supported by priests, campaigned against the idea. It was feared then that the spread of English, at the expense of Italian, would weaken the power of the Church and encourage Protestantism.

It was this controversy that led to the rise of the first Maltese political groups. The campaign against the promotion of English was successful enough to delay the proposed changes for many years. For a long time, both English and Italian were offered as the language of instruction in elementary schools. Parents opted for one or the other. In the 1930s the teaching of Italian was abolished by the British. The Maltese government was suspended soon after it attempted to reintroduce Italian.
The issue only came to an end with the outbreak of World War II, which brought Italy into conflict with Malta.

THE MEDIA

There are daily and weekly newspapers in English and in Maltese. British daily newspapers arrive on the evening of their day of publication, and American newspapers such as *The International Herald Tribune* are also available. Malta Television launched in 1962, five years after the islanders started receiving television signals from Italy. Italian channels remain popular. The first private broadcasting licenses were granted to the two major political parties and the Catholic Church. More stations followed, and there is now a proliferation of privately run radio stations and several television channels. Since Malta is a member of the Council of Europe, media laws are based on European law. Cable television was introduced in 1992 and satellite television is widely watched.

Malta has one public television channel, which broadcasts mostly in Maltese but includes some news and other programs in English, and numerous radio channels. Tall television antennas and satellite dishes are a common sight because of the popularity of Italian television stations, which broadcast extensive coverage of Italian soccer games and also transmit programs that would not generally be shown on the more conservative and Church-influenced state television station. Many of Malta's newspapers and broadcasters have strong political affiliations.

A newspaper kiosk by the bay supplies news to local Maltese.

ARTS

This barrel-vaulted cailing of Saint John's
Co-cathedral is covered in a series of 18 episodes
in the life of Saint John the Baptist, painted by
Mattia Preti, while the pavement floor is made up
of marble tombstones of the Knights of Saint John.

SOME OF THE FINEST ART that Malta has produced is prehistoric, expressed in stone and found in the great megalithic temples that were built before the pyramids of Egypt. They represent some of the world's earliest surviving examples of art. Well over 4,000 years separate this era from the next remarkable expression of artistry in Malta, when the Knights of Saint John arrived in the 16th century and a second great period of building took place.

Artistic pieces of glass shown in a shop in Mosta.

The making of lace with intricate patterns is another contemporary art form, but one that has an ancient lineage in Malta. Lace is made by the local women, particularly in Gozo, where women sit on their doorsteps skillfully plying the bobbins to produce their wares.

The word *megalithic*, which is derived from the ancient Greek words for "large" and "stone," is especially apt in describing Malta's temples because some of their stones weigh over 22 tons (20 metric tons). One megalith measures 23 by 10 feet (7 by 3 m).

GGANTIJA The two temples at Ggantija in Gozo, which date from around 3500 B.C., are believed to be the oldest freestanding monuments in the world. They were built as places to worship a fertility goddess, and it has been suggested that the structures were shaped to represent the head and breasts of the goddess. In the doorway of the larger temple, the holes for the hinges that held a giant set of doors can still be seen. A forecourt area stands in front of this doorway, dividing the congregation from the priests, who may have conducted their ceremonies inside.

Excavations in the early 19th century unearthed various pottery and statuettes, including a rare relief carving of a snake. These are now on display in museums in Valletta and Victoria. Legend has it that this temple was built by a female giant, which ties in with evidence of ritual worship of female fertility figures.

The Ggantija temples. Legend credits the construction of the temples to Sansuna, a female giant. Able to carry huge stones on her head from a local quarry, Sansuna was believed to get her strength from her vegetarian diet.

TARXIEN TEMPLES There are three temples at Tarxien. One of them, known as the South Temple, has a central paved square surrounded by carved stone benches. This area may have been the site for ritual fires, as the burned remains of animal bones have been excavated. A similar design characterizes the earliest of the three temples, the Central Temple, which dates from about 2400 B.C.

In one of the side rooms of this temple, there is a huge bowl that was carved from a single piece of stone. The art of this Stone Age society is revealed in various relief carvings of spirals and animals—cattle, pigs, goats, and bulls—that decorate some of the walls. At both Tarxien and other temple sites the most intriguing finds are various headless figures, known as the "fat" deities because of their obese appearance.

HAGAR QIM AND MNAJDRA TEMPLE Hagar Qim is a fan-like series of oval rooms that archaeologists believe were not conceived as a single project but were added on at different times. As at Ggantija, holes have been found around the entrance where the hinges of doors once fit, again suggesting a clear division between priests and ordinary participants at temple ceremonies. Both Hagar Qim and Mnajdra, situated nearby in a more sheltered position, reveal evidence of early humans' artistic endeavors—patterns of pitted and spiral designs cut into stone.

THE HYPOGEUM A hypogeum is an underground chamber. When several Maltese house builders accidentally broke through the roof of one in 1902, they tried to keep it a secret because they knew the authorities would delay the construction of the house they were working on. It was a few years before the secret was revealed. Then, when the site was excavated, it was found to consist of three levels of catacombs.

One was a naturally occurring structure, while the other two had been carved out of the soft limestone. They were used as burial chambers, but their greatest significance is as monumental works of art. They have survived for five millennia, as have the spiral and hexagonal designs that decorated the walls and pillars. However, they were closed to the public for many years after the discovery that the carbon dioxide breathed out by thousands of visitors every week was beginning to unsettle the delicate climatic balance of the underground environment.

The bones of about 7,000 people have been found in the Hypogeum, together with various artifacts. The Hypogeum has stood the test of time—it was used as an air-raid shelter in World War II, some 5,000 years after its construction, before mass tourism began to threaten its structural integrity.

ART OF THE KNIGHTS

The great art of Malta associated with the Knights of Saint John was not the creative work of individual members of the Order. What was important was the wealth and power of the Knights, for they represented the cream of European aristocracy and used their great wealth to commission the best architects and artists to work for them. Their legacy can be found today in the unique design and architecture of Valletta, the stately palazzos (Italian mansions) they commissioned, the auberges (inns) they lived in, and most magnificently of all, their baroque cathedrals and other churches.

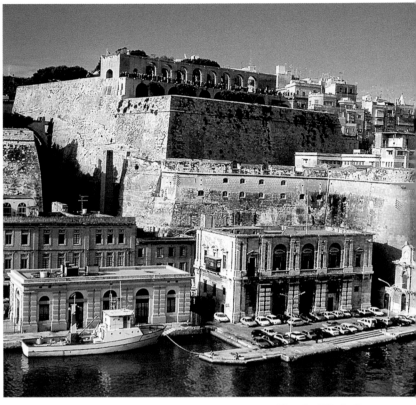

The fortified city of Valletta is perhaps the most enduring legacy of the Knights of Saint John.

Work started on the construction of Valletta soon after the end of the Great Siege in 1565. Several important architects, mostly Italian, were involved, but the initial design was the work of Francesco Laparelli da Cortona (1521—70). It was he who proposed the building of a completely new city. Laparelli devised a grid system based on eight main streets running from the northwest to the southeast, and intersected by 10 other streets that were laid out perpendicularly to the main streets. The open sea protected one end of Valletta, while a huge ditch was built outside the main entrance at the other inland end and massive fortifications were built to defend it. These deep walls still stand today, despite heavy bombing in the area during World War II.

Laparelli died of the plague before the work was completed and his Maltese assistant, Gerolamo Cassar (1520—86), took over. Cassar was to become responsible for many of the important buildings erected by the Order, including Saint John's Co-cathedral.

The lush interior of Saint Paul's Cathedral.

SAINT JOHN'S CO-CATHEDRAL

The rather austere exterior of this church, completed in 1578, gives little indication of the incredible wealth of art that decorates the interior. The floor of the nave is composed of some 400 tombs of noted Knights. Many of the tombs are highly individual in their design. Highly ornate side chapels branch off from the central nave, each one dedicated to one of the European nations from which the Knights came. The Chapel of Germany has a beautiful white marble altar, while the Chapel of Italy used to contain a famous painting by Caravaggio, *Saint Jerome*, which was stolen in 1984 but recovered a few years later. It is now in the secure church museum, next to another Caravaggio painting, *The Beheading of Saint John the Baptist* (*opposite page*). The Chapel of Aragon is one of the most artistic areas in the cathedral and contains a number of paintings by Mattia Preti, as well as very ornate memorial stones.

SAINT PAUL'S CATHEDRAL

Building work started on this magnificent church, a minor masterpiece of European church architecture, in 1697 and was completed five years later.

ART GALORE

The single most important artist commissioned by the Knights was Caravaggio (1571—1610), one of the greatest Italian artists, who arrived in Malta in 1607. He was glad to leave Italy, where he was wanted for murder, and later became a knight in Malta. After completing several paintings he became involved in a fight and was expelled from the Order. He returned to Italy, where,

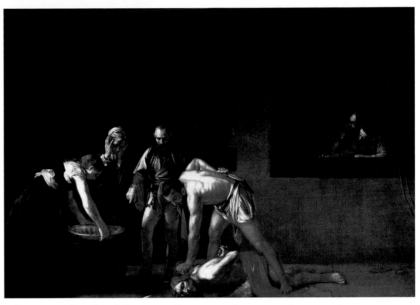

while waiting for a pardon from the Pope, he died from malaria at the age of 38. He is noted for using ordinary working people as models for his religious paintings. Saint John's Co-cathedral also contains a set of highly artistic Flemish tapestries, which were modeled on drawings by the famous Flemish artist, Rubens.

Other fine works of art include sculptures by the Maltese Antonio Sciortino and paintings by the Venetian Domenico Tintoretto, a relative of the famous Tintoretto, and by Antoine de Favray, the French artist.

The exterior is made up of three bays, each with its own door and divided by pillars. There are two bell towers. The interior is a tribute to Maltese baroque art. The 164-foot-long (50-m-long) nave is paved with marble tombstones of notable members of society of the time, and although they are all largely forgotten today, their splendid memorial stones remain as testimony to the artisans who created them. Similar tombs are found in the side chapels.

There are also a number of valuable individual works of art inside the church, including frescoes and paintings, a 15th-century marble font, and a carved door to the sacristy made of solid Irish oak. This door is part of an older church that was destroyed in an earthquake in 1693.

The Gobelin Tapestries in the Grand Master's Palace were based on a set of paintings by two artists who had traveled to South America and Africa in the 17th century.

THE AUBERGES

The Knights who first arrived in Malta were divided into groups according to their nationalities, and each group built its own "inn of residence." *Auberge* is a French word meaning "inn," and the various homes of the Knights came to be known by this name. Nine auberges were built, seven of which were designed by Gerolamo Cassar between 1571 and 1575, though only four still stand today.

One of the most artistic, which was home to Knights from parts of Spain and Portugal, is the Auberge of Castile. It has three rows of windows, with scroll and shell ornamentation, and a highly ornate doorway flanked by cannons and decorated with a bust of a grand master amid an array of banners and triumphal insignia. Although bombed and damaged during World War II, it has been carefully restored and is now the office of the prime minister.

The Auberge of Italy is another fine example of the artistic architecture that the Knights were able to commission. The imposing facade contains a bust of another grand master and his escutcheon (a shield or emblem bearing a coat of arms).

THE GRAND MASTER'S PALACE

Some of the more artistic buildings in Malta are Italian-style palazzos. They were commissioned by the Order and one of them, the Palazzo di Citta, built as a public records office in 1720, is still used for that purpose today. But for artistic achievement, few can compare with the Grand Master's Palace in Valletta. It was built in 1569 as a prestigious house for a grand master's nephew and was extended two years later by Gerolamo Cassar. It now occupies an entire block in the capital and houses Malta's House of Representatives.

Many of the rooms are decorated with friezes portraying events from the history of the Order and impressive portraits of various grand masters through the centuries. One painting is by Mateo Perez d'Aleccio, a student of Michelangelo. There is also an armory with extensive examples of armor and weaponry.

Perhaps the most important work of art, however, is a set of tapestries that adorn the walls of one room. The tapestries consist of 10 large panels depicting colorful animals and birds and are known as the Gobelin Tapestries after a famous factory in Paris where they were made after being commissioned by a grand master.

THE MANOEL THEATER

This beautiful, baroque theater was named after the grand master of the time, a Portuguese named Antonio Manoel de Vilhena. The theater is the third-oldest in the world. It is still in use, and as Malta's national theater, it hosts the more important plays and concerts. The Manoel Theater was built between 1722 and 1736, a time when the Knights were experiencing one of their more peaceful periods and were eager to enjoy the social activities and forms of entertainment that a theater could facilitate.

Although an inscription over the door proclaims that it was built for "the honest recreation of the people," it was reserved for the ruling class of Knights, and ordinary Maltese would not have visited the place. The theater fell into disuse in the 1860s and was later used as a hostel for the poor and then a movie theater, but was restored in the 1960s. Today its interior is

The entrance to the Grand Master's Palace.

Above: **The interior of the magnificent dome-shaped Manoel Theater.**

Opposite: Les Gavroches or Street Urchins, **by Antonio Sciortino in upper Barrakka Gardens in Valletta.**

stunning. The stage area is small and the stalls seat fewer than 300 people, but rising above them are three tiers of baroque boxes in gold and green and decorated with frescoes. Above the boxes is a gallery area, where one can even reach out and touch the gilded ceiling, which gives some indication of the intimacy of the theater.

CONTEMPORARY ART

The works of contemporary Maltese artists include paintings, prints, sculpture, jewelry, and couture. One well-known artist in Malta is Norbert Attard, whose early work includes prints of abstract geometric shapes against a spray-brushed background and who has now moved on to installation art. Joe Xuereb is a sculptor from Gozo, while Joseph Bellia is a landscape painter from the island of Malta. One of the most famous Maltese artists—and one with an international reputation—is Alfred Chircop. Sue and Anna Nightingale, mother and daughter, form a painting duo from Gozo. Their work embraces both pictorial subjects and abstract themes.

LITERATURE AND PATRIOTISM

Malta's literary tradition only started in the 19th century. Writers who have emerged include Dun Karm, the most notable Maltese poet. Three moments in Maltese history recur as popular themes in Maltese literature and all three record the overcoming of an external threat—the defeat of Turkish invaders, the expulsion of Napoleon's troops in 1800, and the islands' heroic stand against aerial bombardment in World War II. The frequency with which these events are referred to suggests the importance of these moments in shaping and giving expression to Maltese national pride.

ORAL POETRY

There is still a tradition of reciting poetry in Malta, and this remains a popular form of entertainment. Known as *ghana* (ANN-aa), the term covers a variety of poems that are sung to the musical accompaniment of guitars. Sometimes they are performed by two singers who recite their verses as if they were competing against each other. Another version takes the form of a long and complicated narrative based on the exploits of legendary figures or even contemporary events. A typical poem is a rhyming four-line verse, with each line usually having eight syllables.

This traditional art form has been given a new lease on life by young folk singers and musicians who use modern technology to record these traditional poems.

LEISURE

Locals enjoying a stroll along an
old street in Valletta.

MALTA IS NOT A workaholic society and leisure time is not some precious commodity that has to be snatched from the timetable of a busy day. Leisure takes its natural place alongside the world of work and they complement, rather than compete with, each other. This is especially apparent in the refreshing practice of taking a casual stroll with a partner or a friend when the heat of the afternoon sun has subsided.

The beaches at Mellieha Bay are popular with the Maltese and tourists alike.

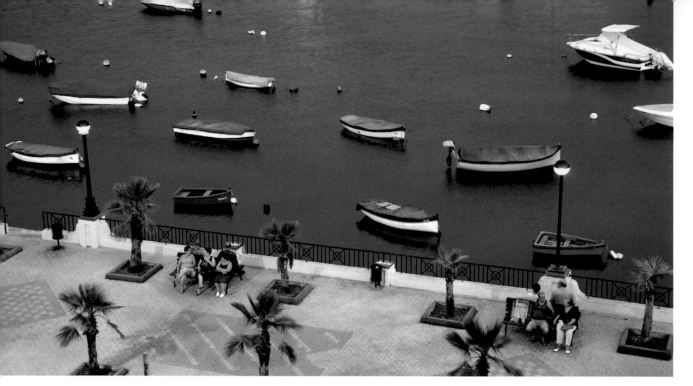

Families taking a break at the benches next to the marina bay. Strolling along the waterfront is an enjoyable leisure activity for many Maltese.

STROLLING IN THE STREET

This traditional feature of the Maltese lifestyle, that of dressing up in stylish clothes—but never overdressing—and going out for a social walk, helps define the difference between a Mediterranean culture as found in countries such as Malta and the more work-oriented, faster-paced lifestyle of Northern Europe.

Older people tend to walk in pairs, with their partner, relative, or friend, while younger people usually move in small groups. The activity provides an opportunity for informal conversation and a possible encounter with friends or neighbors who are also out walking. In towns, certain streets and routes, often the promenade that follows the course of the shoreline, are popular.

The early evening stroll is an endearing habit of the Maltese, not least because it suggests a relaxed state of mind that can enjoy a simple social act such as walking with a friend for no specific purpose. In rural areas, where there are no paved promenades, the village square takes on the same social function. In the early summer evening, when people have refreshed themselves after a siesta, the pavement corners around the square and the outdoor tables of cafés become gathering points for exchanging news.

PARK LIFE

The municipal park is a familiar part of urban life and nowhere is this more true than in Malta, especially on the weekends. Malta's relaxed and unhurried pace of life, combined with the strong role of the family in most people's lives, help to make the public park a microcosm of national life.

One of the biggest parks is Buskett Gardens near Rabat, with its large wooded grounds. It was designed by Gerolamo Cassar in the late 16th century and was once part of the official summer residence of the British governor. Except in the winter, it is popular with picnicking families and young couples. Every year at the end of June the park is the site of a popular folk festival, Mnarja (the feast of Saint Peter and Saint Paul).

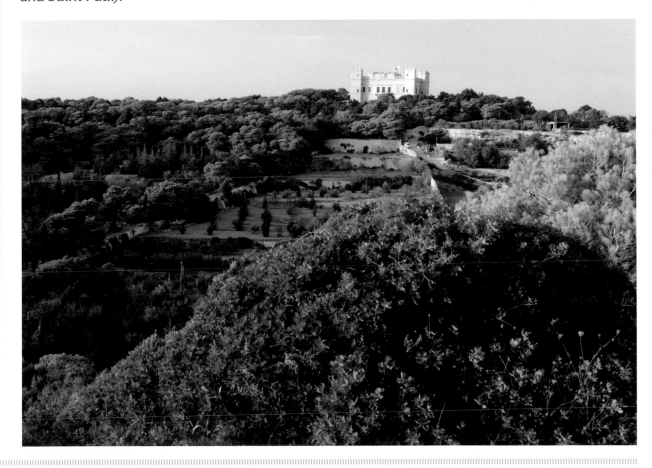

The Malta Marathon, first held in 1986, has become an established annual event for the Maltese as well as hundreds of runners from around the world.

SOCCER

The most popular sport in Malta is soccer. The game was first introduced to the country by the British, and the tremendous popularity of the sport across Europe, especially in nearby Italy, has assured it a place in Maltese culture. In most countries, soccer clubs compete with one another in different leagues, according to their level of ability, but because Malta has such a small population the same small number of teams tends to achieve success each year.

The limited pool of talent also affects Malta's ability to form an international team capable of competing effectively with other national teams in Europe and North Africa. Although Malta rarely achieves international success, this has not diminished the people's enormous interest in soccer. As it is possible to receive Italian television programs, Italian league games, generally representing some of the most skillful soccer in the world, can be seen in the homes of ordinary Maltese.

Satellite television also offers live English soccer games. A regular Maltese soccer enthusiast is as familiar with top clubs such as Manchester United from England and Juventus from Italy as supporters in those countries would be.

Maltese children enjoying a game of street soccer.

Maltese families enjoying a day at a water park.

OTHER SPORTS

Water-based sports such as swimming, water polo, waterskiing, windsurfing, and sailing are also popular with the Maltese. Most of the country's land-based sports, apart from soccer, take place at the Marsa. This large flat area was where the Turks set up base during the Great Siege of 1565. It is now the site of the country's major sports club and where Malta's second-most popular sport, horse-racing, takes place.

Between October and May, weekly race meetings, including trotting races, are held. Trotting races—short and fast races using a pony (a smaller breed of horse), or even a donkey, harnessed to a small, compact vehicle called a sulky—are enormously popular, and many Maltese bet on them. Maltese teenagers prefer to spend their leisure time at the large ten-pin bowling alley and roller rink complex on Malta Island.

Fishing is popular with men, although it is enjoyed more as a form of relaxation than as an active sport. As a fishing license is not required, the activity is popular with casual fishermen. The rods used are unusually long because the best fish do not swim close to the shore. Enthusiasts have to clamber out onto the edges of rocky points to get as far out to the sea as possible.

Other sports enjoyed by the Maltese include horse riding, golf, tennis, squash, badminton, field hockey, basketball, polo, and archery. Golf in Malta dates back to 1888, when the game was introduced by the British governor. Polo is a stick-and-ball game played on horseback by two teams of four. Points are scored by hitting the ball with a handheld mallet into the opposing team's goal, and each game is divided into a series of seven-minute periods known as chukkas. The game has its origins in central Asia. The water-based version, water polo, was developed by the British in the 19th century and is played in swimming pools. Both sports were introduced into Malta by the British.

KILLING FIELDS

After a long history of illegal bird killing, the Maltese government finally has been ordered by the European Court of Justice in January 2008 not to allow the hunting and trapping of birds any longer—a practice that is in direct contravention of European bird protection laws. In a verdict delivered the

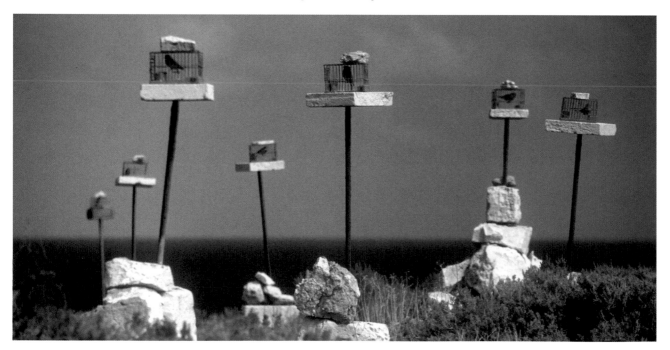

Caged birds kept to attract wild birds for sport shooting in Malta.

THE GAMBLING PASSION

Betting is a national pastime and takes various forms, the most popular being lotteries. A familiar sight in any town is a small trestle table and a vendor holding a roll of lottery tickets for sale. At the most local level a lottery prize may be only a household item, with the profits going to the village fund to finance the annual festival. Some prizes, however, can be very substantial and the results are published in the newspapers and broadcast on television. Gambling also takes the form of local bingo sessions, held in a hall or movie theater, while more serious gamblers can patronize Malta's casino.

week of September 11, 2009, the European Court of Justice declared that Malta breached European law by allowing spring hunting of turtle dove and quail in the years 2004—7. This ruling has been welcomed by conservation groups who still remain concerned about illegal hunting of protected species in Malta (such as raptors and herons), and a lack of adequate police enforcement.

About 5 percent of the population, mostly men, used to look forward to spring and fall each year when they could gather in fields, public parks, and other places to shoot as many small birds as possible. Sparrows, finches, song birds, and up to 100,000 birds of prey, including more than 30,000 kestrels, became victims in the mass slaughters that used to take place annually. It has been estimated that 10 million cartridges used to be fired each year.

Enthusiasts defended this unusual pastime as an ancient tradition in Malta. Not all Maltese, however, accepted this argument. In the late 1990s, a book on the subject written by a Maltese conservationist was published: *Fatal Flight—The Maltese Obsession with Killing Birds*. In it the author pointed out that when Malta became a member nation of the European Union it would no longer be able to condone this practice of bird-killing. Although Malta joined the European Union in 2004, it still allowed the hunting and trapping of turtle doves and quail every spring in direct contravention of the EU birds directive, which seeks to protect, manage, and regulate all bird species naturally living in the wild within the European territory of the member states, including the eggs of these birds, their nests, and their habitats.

The Maltese islands lie on the central European-African migration flyway used by millions of birds each spring and fall. A total of 384 bird species have been recorded in Malta. A recent study analyzing ring recoveries in Malta, showed that birds originating from a minimum of 36 European countries have been recorded migrating over Malta.

FESTIVALS

Colorful and beautifully decorated floats have become one of the main attractions of Carnival.

MALTA'S CAPACITY FOR ENJOYING festive occasions is most apparent in the plethora of *festi* (FEST-e) that punctuate the social calendar between May and September.

The *festa* (FEST-a), or feast, has its origins in the religious traditions of village communities. The setting aside of at least one day each year to honor the village church's patron saint has become the occasion for each village and town to celebrate its own sense of communal identity.

FESTI

Preparing for a village *festa* is often a hectic activity because of the competition among neighboring villages to mount a more colorful and more exciting event. *Festa* events are scheduled well in advance and are meticulously planned to ensure that everything runs smoothly.

Celebrations take place over at least one weekend, and apart from the solemn church services and religious processions, there are numerous secular events that lend a nonreligious flavor to every *festa*. Indeed, for a growing number of Maltese, a visit to the church to appreciate the displays and ornamentation may be the only time in the year that they step

A Maltese man and woman in their masquerade costume during Carnival. The country's many festivals are celebrated with a great deal of enthusiasm by the Maltese.

Festi are noisy, exuberant affairs and a big tourist draw.

inside their local church. The social and festive nature of the *festa* is reflected in the tremendous noise that accompanies such festivals, with every village announcing the imminent arrival of their festival by setting off fireworks.

The notion behind these pre-*festa* celebrations seems to be that the louder the noise, the more confidence the villagers have that their *festa* will be more glamorous than the previous year and more successful and popular than their neighboring village's event. Complementing the noise is the display of multicolored fireworks exploding across the sky. The drama is heightened by the thousands of small colored bulbs strung across streets and hung from public and private buildings.

A highlight of the festival is the processional march of a band, followed by a crowd of local people enjoying the atmosphere. The occasion is a unique blend of the formal and the informal because the musicians make impromptu stops along the way, pausing for complimentary refreshments. The climax takes place on Sunday when the statue of the patron saint is paraded through the streets, confetti is thrown from the windows of houses along the route, and fireworks light up the sky. At the end of the day, when the streets are empty, it can look like there has been a sudden downpour of colored snow because the pavements are literally carpeted in confetti.

Malta's fireworks displays are said to be among the finest to be seen anywhere in Europe. Today the Malta International Fireworks Festival is held on the night of April 30 and May 1, partly to commemorate Malta's entrance into the European Union on May 1, 2004.

The origins of the festa go back to the 16th century when the local nobility would play the part of the honorable patron. Once a year the local landowner would finance a small celebration to gain the goodwill of the peasants. Over time a sense of competition gradually developed between the landowners as some of them used the celebrations to display their generosity and power. Gifts of money to the local church were used to finance the purchase of a statue of the patron saint. The combined influence of the nobility and the Church gradually involved the peasants more and more.

By the early 18th century a form of fireworks was used for the first time. A decisive factor in the development of the festival was the growing involvement of the Knights as the Order of Saint John recognized the value of the celebrations in raising the morale of the poor. It was the wealth of the Order that transformed these minor festivals into spectacular events. Then the British arrived on the scene with their military bands and pomp and ceremony. They encouraged villages to form their own bands because they too saw the value of helping the peasants forget their poverty for at least a few days.

Today the organization and financing of village festivals is managed completely at the local level. There is no government subsidy. The rich still play a significant role in financing the celebrations and often donate lavish bouquets of flowers for decorating the statue of the patron saint.

CARNIVAL

This was once a religious festival that preceded the first day of Lent, traditionally a period of fasting that leads up to Easter. The beginnings of this Maltese festival, however, date back much further than Christianity. The festival has its origins in a pagan celebration to mark the end of winter, and the highlight of this week-long event is a procession of colorful floats that sets off just outside Valletta and makes its way through the gates of the city and into the capital. Some of the more artistic floats take the form of giant displays of flowers carefully laid out on the back of an open truck. Even more time-consuming to design and make are the striking costumes that appear in the parade.

During Carnival, Malta's main nightlife center, Paceville, catches the late-night Carnival goers who pile into the clubs and bars, still wearing their outrageous outfits.

Locals performing during Carnival.

Around the same time of the year, the island of Gozo holds a similar festive event, and although it is held on a much smaller scale, it shares with the Valletta festival historical roots based on a primitive celebration of the approach of spring.

MNARJA

The feast of Saint Peter and Saint Paul on June 29 is a public holiday and the occasion for an important festival traditionally known as Mnarja (im-NAAR-ya), from a Maltese word meaning "light." Its origins are lost in time, but it may have been a country folk festival that has survived into modern times. This feast has always been considered a special day for everyone, particularly for the peasants who used to have their annual break at this time of year and tried to enjoy it to the fullest. The traditional start to the festival occurs some days before the event with a formal procession of Boy Scouts from the city of Mdina, accompanied by a band and members of the organizing committee, who carry and display the prizes that will later be awarded to winners of the horse races that will take place on June 29.

In the old days, it was customary for a town crier to herald the holding of Mnarja by reading a proclamation at certain parts of the city of Mdina.

BAND CLUBS

It would be difficult to imagine a Maltese festival that did not include the presence of a brass band. The bands' significance to the national culture has been recognized by the government, which plans to promote their popularity so that they do not die out like other cultural traditions. Band clubs have also been recognized as a useful way to encourage a love of music among the young.

Malta has more than 84 bands, including a police band. The various bands attract about 4,000 bandsmen/women (bandisti), more than a quarter of whom are women. The oldest band clubs can trace their history back to the late 19th century. In 1999 the Saint Philip band club of Zebbug (ZE-booje) triumphantly announced that documents had been found proving their band was set up in 1851.

On the eve of the 29th, the festivities move to Buskett Gardens on the outskirts of Rabat, where an agricultural show is already bustling with activity. Some people will spend the night in the gardens, camping under the trees, and the sound of bands and Spanish guitars is heard until the early hours of the morning.

On the day of the 29th, attention switches back to Mdina, where traditional horse and donkey races take place. An amusing feature of these races is that the animals are ridden bareback and the jockeys have to grip their mounts with their knees, while driving the animals forward with a short stick. In the 17th and 18th centuries, special races were held for slaves until they were abolished by Napoleon in 1798. After the races the prizes are distributed, an ancient tradition that goes back at least three centuries, according to a Latin motto inscribed on the walls of the city: *Cuicumque legitime certaverit* ("For all who lawfully strive to win").

Fireworks designs being set off in a festival on Gozo island.

A Good Friday procession in Malta.

CHRISTMAS

Unlike the celebrations in many other European countries, Christmas in Malta is far less of a public festival and much less commercial in spirit. This is mainly because of the traditional religious significance that is still attached to Christmas. Familiar practices include the decorating of streets and buildings with colored lights and community groups singing carols in public places. Christmas trees are also decorated and placed in the windows of homes and gifts are exchanged between friends and family members, but there is little of the shopping frenzy seen in some European cities in the weeks and days leading up to Christmas.

December 25 is essentially a family celebration. Shops and businesses are all closed. One of the busiest places is the arrival hall of Malta's only international airport as many Maltese working and living abroad return home to be with their families.

HOLY WEEK

Holy Week marks the religious celebrations leading up to Easter Sunday. As compared with most other festive occasions it is a somber event, commemorating the death and resurrection of Jesus Christ. It starts on the Friday of the week before the Easter weekend with a major procession through the streets of Valletta and smaller processions in other towns.

On the following Thursday, traditional "Last Supper" displays are held in religious institutions in some towns, commemorating the last meal of Christ and his apostles, as described in the New Testament of the Bible. A traditional

Many of Malta's public holidays mark religious events. The few exceptions either celebrate nationalist events or commemorate workers' rights:

January 1	*New Year's Day*
February 10	*Saint Paul's Shipwreck*
March 19	*Saint Joseph's Day*
March 31	*Freedom Day*
April	*Good Friday*
May 1	*Workers' Day*
June 7	*Commemoration of 1919 Riot*
June 29	*Feast of Saints Peter and Paul*
August 15	*The Assumption of Our Lady into Heaven*
September 8	*Great Siege of Victories (Our Lady of Victories)*
September 21	*Independence Day*
December 8	*Feast of the Immaculate Conception*
December 13	*Republic Day*
December 25	*Christmas Day*

display features a table prepared for Christ and his 12 apostles with fresh loaves, wine jars, and pastries.

The next day is Good Friday, the day that traditionally marks the crucifixion of Christ. Good Friday is a public holiday and all businesses and entertainment outlets are closed. Processions with life-sized statues depicting scenes associated with the biblical event take place in many towns.

Easter Sunday is a day of celebration, marking the Christian belief that on this day Christ was resurrected. Like Christmas Day, this is very much a family occasion. Relatives and friends visit one another's houses, and Easter eggs are presented to children. A special sweet, the *figolla* (FIG-ole-ar), a pastry cut into various shapes such as the Maltese Cross, is prepared for this day. It is filled with marzipan and covered with colored icing.

A Christmas highlight, popular among children and adults alike, is the annual pantomime held at the Manoel Theater in Valletta, the third-oldest working theater in Europe.

FOOD

Stocks of fresh fruits and vegetables being sold at the markets in Valletta.

MALTESE FOOD, like its history, owes much to various foreign cultures. Obvious examples of this are pasta, introduced from Italy, and British fare such as fish and chips. The first appearance of British food may have its origins in colonial history, but the annual invasion by hundreds of thousands of vacationers from Britain has helped popularize some of these dishes in restaurants and, indirectly, in the homes of Maltese families.

Horse meat was fairly widely eaten in the past when available, usually steamed, fried with garlic, or simmered on top of the stove or in the oven in an onion and white wine sauce.

Many of the more fashionable restaurants in Malta today are influenced by Italian or French cuisine. However, Malta also has a distinctive Maltese cuisine that, like its language, has managed to survive and prosper, despite centuries of foreign domination.

MALTESE FOOD

Maltese food is the product of a rural society, but the country's climate and ecology has also made a significant contribution. Many vegetables can be grown throughout the year and are readily available to all families.

Fresh fish for sale at the Sunday market in Marsaxlokk.

A nougat stall in Valetta. The Maltese have a sweet tooth, and cakes and cookies are popular snacks.

Yet another traditional vegetable soup is *kusksu* (kus-KSUE), made from broad beans with pasta and tomatoes.

The scarcity of firewood for ovens in the days when electricity or gas was not commonly available accounts for the tradition of cooking food slowly in earthenware pots.

In the past it was not unusual to take food to the village baker to be roasted in his oven after the bread had been taken out for the day. Although modern technology has eliminated the need to do this, this style of cooking continues to influence the nature and taste of traditional dishes. Even the tradition of taking food to the baker has not died out completely—on Sundays this can still be observed in some villages in Gozo.

A rural lifestyle and the fact that in the past the majority of Maltese were not well-off also accounts for the popularity of soups. Because the vegetables are grown locally, a glut of some types of vegetables occurs now and then. This reduces their price and encourages people to combine their flavors over slow cooking. *Minestra* (MIN-ess-traa), a type of minestrone, is often prepared for lunch or as a first course for an evening meal, but depending on the quantity and type of ingredients, it can easily become a filling meal in itself.

Another vegetable dish is *soppa tal armla* (SOP-pah taal AM-laa), which is quite different in character and taste from the bulky and chunky minestra. Instead of using thick portions of six to 10 different ingredients, *soppa tal armla* uses only white and green vegetables and is traditionally served with goat cheese. *Aljotta* (AL-yacht-ta), a light broth made from fish, is especially popular in the summer months when fish is plentiful.

NATIONAL DISHES

Fenek (fe-NECK), or rabbit, is one of Malta's most popular and distinctive dishes. It is eaten stewed, roasted, or fried. The origins of this dish are not difficult to understand, for when families were poor and food was scarce, it was always possible to hunt or trap a rabbit. Nowadays, wild rabbits may no longer be abundant in the countryside, but the popularity of rabbit as a dish has not diminished and rabbits are reared especially for the kitchen.

Another national dish is *lampuka* (lam-POO-ka), which is actually a seasonal swordfish called the *dorado* (door-add-o). The fish is relatively easy for local fishermen to catch with nets. The swordfish is fried or baked in a pie with olives, cauliflower, spinach, chestnuts, and raisins. Almost as popular is *bragioli* (BRA-geo-lee), tiny parcels of stuffing wrapped in slices of beef and cooked slowly at low temperature.

MALTESE BREAD

A Maltese light meal of *hobz-bi-zejt* (bruschetta-style bread with oil), with tomatoes, capers, garlic and pepper *gbejnet* (cheese).

The mass-produced bread that is sold in supermarkets is a far cry from the traditional Maltese bread. Sour-dough Maltese bread is baked on the surface of an oven that gives it a firm crust but with a soft, light center. The customary way to eat the bread is by adding olive oil, hence its name *hobz biz-zejt* (hops BIZ-zeyt), which translates simply as "bread with oil." Tomatoes are first rubbed onto a slice of the bread, coloring it naturally. Peppers and capers are then added, before finally pouring on the olive oil.

Ftira (FEER-tee-rah) is a low-rise, ring-shaped, small, less-crusty Maltese bread that is usually baked in a very hot oven. In Gozo, *ftira* filled with sardines or anchovies was a typical supper snack during Lent fast days, when eating meat was not allowed.

FAST FOOD

Fast food has found its way to Malta and does not just cater to tourists. In fashionable areas such as Sliema, numerous small restaurants serve burgers, pizza, and Chinese food in plastic containers. An American fast-food chain that first opened in Valletta in 1995 now has an outlet for every 45,000 people, giving Malta the highest market penetration in the world outside of the United States.

Food   **127**

Perhaps because the Knights of Malta prohibited the islanders from eating rabbit, except when the feast of Saints Peter and Paul was held at the end of June, or maybe because most Maltese families kept rabbits as courtyard animals destined for the pot, rabbit is very popular and one of the best-known Maltese dishes, one of the few served in restaurants. The rabbit, often previously marinated, is lightly browned with garlic and herbs, then simmered for several hours, ideally in a terracotta casserole, in red wine or a rich tomato sauce. Restaurants usually serve it with fries and salad, although crusty local bread to soak up the rich sauces and a cooked green vegetable are more appropriate. Traditionally rabbit stew is served on spaghetti. The meal based on spaghetti with rabbit and rabbit stew is called fenkata *(from* fenek, *meaning "rabbit") and for many it is the national dish. The tradition of enjoying* fenkata *on the feast day of Saint Peter and Saint Paul continues today.*

But Malta had its own local fast food long before the now familiar franchises first appeared. Known as *pastizzi* (PAST-TITS-see), these are flaky pastry snacks with a savory taste best enjoyed when warm and fresh. They are sometimes, mistakenly, translated as "cheesecakes" because cheese is the most common filling, but they taste little like the sweet North American cheesecake.

PASTA

Maltese families do not eat pasta as frequently as Italians do, but the dish is enormously popular, both in the home and in restaurants. Two of the most popular traditional dishes are baked pasta—*timpana* (TIM-paa-nah) and *mqarrun fil-forn* (IM-ah-roon ill-fourn). Both dishes are made of macaroni with layers of meat, cheese, tomatoes, and eggs, while *timpana* is wrapped in light pastry.

DESSERTS

There are a number of traditional Maltese desserts. Nougat and hot, date-stuffed fried fritters are popular. Another favorite, usually eaten at the end of a meal with tea or coffee, is *kannoli* (can-OH-lee), a tube-shaped confection of deep-fried crisp pastry filled with a mixture of fresh-whipped cream, small pieces of candied fruit and chocolate, and ricotta cheese. A light dusting of powdered sugar and pistachios complete this delicacy, which originated in Sicily.

A selection of Maltese wines.

DRINKS

It is thought that the Phoenicians first brought the skill of making wine to Malta and that the process was revived in the 17th century by the Knights of Saint John. Today local grapes are used to produce wines that carry floral and fruity flavors. The strongest wines are produced on Gozo by small family enterprises.

The Maltese are not heavy beer drinkers, although there is a popular beer called Cisk (CHISK) that is brewed on the island. There is also a popular non-alcoholic drink called Kinnie, which is made using herbs that give it a distinctive taste. Malta also produces a liquor called *bajtra* (BITE-trah) from the fruit of the prickly pear cactus. It has a bright pink color and a sweet taste.

TIMPANA (MACARONI PIE)

4 servings

4 ounces (110 grams or ½ cup) chopped onions

Clove of garlic

Olive oil

1 pound (500 g) ground beef

4 ounces (110 g) chicken liver

¾ cup (180 ml) peeled tomatoes

4 tablespoons (60 ml) tomato paste

Salt and pepper

½ cup (125 ml) water

1½ pounds (700 g) macaroni

2 hard-boiled eggs

4 tablespoons (60 ml) grated Parmesan cheese

1½ pounds (700 g) short crust or puff pastry dough

4 eggs, beaten (for egg wash)

- Fry the onion and garlic in olive oil. Add ground beef and liver and brown for several minutes. Add tomatoes and tomato paste. Season with salt and pepper. Let it cook for a few seconds, then slowly add water and simmer until meat is tender, for about 20 minutes.

- Meanwhile, boil macaroni, drain, and cool. Chop the hard-boiled eggs and add them to the pasta, along with Parmesan cheese and the meat and sauce mixture.

- Roll pastry into a large, greased baking dish. Pour the macaroni and meat sauce mixture in and cover with dough. Press the edges down to seal the pastry. Pierce the top with a fork, and brush with egg wash.

- Bake for about an hour at 375°F (190°C) or until the dough is golden-brown. Serve hot or cold with grated Parmesan cheese.

FIGOLLA (ALMOND PASTRY)

4 servings

For the pastry:

14 ounces (400 g) margarine

1¾ pound (800 g) flour

7 ounces (200 g) sugar

3 egg yolks

½ teaspoon (2½ ml) grated lemon rind

Water to bind

For the filling:

14 ounces (400 g) sugar

14 ounces (400 g) ground almonds

1 tablespoon (15 ml) orange-flower water

3 egg whites

For the pastry:

- Sieve the flour into a large bowl and rub in the margarine.
- Add sugar and lemon rind.
- Mix in the yolks and enough water to make a stiff dough.
- Allow to rest.

For the filling:

- Prepare the filling by mixing the sugar and the almonds, adding the orange-flower water and folding the beaten egg-whites into this mixture.

Figolla:

- Roll out pastry, and using cookie cutters, cut two similar shapes for each figolla.
- Spread a 0.4-inch-thick (1-cm-thick) layer of the almond filling onto half of the pastry shapes leaving a bit of space around the edges, and cover each one with its corresponding half.
- Press the edges together and bake in a 360°F (180°C) oven until golden for 35 to 40 minutes.
- Allow to cool, cover and decorate with colorful icing or melted chocolate.

	A	B	C	D

1

G O Z O

MEDITERRANEAN SEA

Victoria ● ∴ Ggantija

North Comino Channel

Cominotto   Comino

South Comino Channel

2

Marfa Ridge

Mellieha Bay

St. Paul's Islands

Mellieha ●

Mellieha Ridge

St. Paul's Bay

Bajda Ridge

Wardija Ridge

● Gharghur

Marsamxett Harbor

Victoria Lines Fault

Sliema ●

N

▲ Nadur Tower

● Mosta

Birkirkara ●

Fort St. Elmo

Valletta ●

MALTA

Fort St. Angelo

3

Mdina-Verdala Ridge

● Mdina

Hamrun ●

Grand Harbor

● Rabat

Qormi ●

Marsa ●

● Paola

● Zabbar

∴ Tarxien

Luqa ●

Hypogeum
Of Hal Saflieni

Dingli Cliffs ▲   Buskett Gardens

Marsaxlokk ●

(829 ft/253 m)

Ghar Dalam ∴

Mnajdra ∴   ∴ Hagar Qim

Birzebbuga ●

Marsaxlokk
Bay

4

● Capital city
● Major town
∴ Historical site
▲ Mountain peak

Feet		Meters
1,650		500
660		200
0		0

⌐ Filfla

MAP OF MALTA

ECONOMIC MALTA

Agriculture

 Barley

 Cauliflower

 Grapes

 Green peppers

 Potatoes

 Tomatoes

 Wheat

Services

 Airport

 Port

 Tourism

Natural Resources

 Limestone

 Salt

ABOUT THE ECONOMY

OVERVIEW

The strengths of the economy of Malta are its limestone, a favorable geographic location, and a productive labor force. Malta produces only about 20 percent of its food needs, has limited freshwater supplies, and has no domestic energy sources. The economy is dependent on foreign trade, manufacturing (especially electronics), tourism, and financial services. In 2003 more than 1.2 million tourists visited the island. With a per capita GDP of $23,760 Malta ranks 20th out of 29 European Union (EU) countries in terms of affluence. The island joined the EU in 2004 despite having been divided politically over the question earlier. A sizable budget deficit was a key concern, but initiatives by government have changed the situation enough for the country to be admitted into the Eurozone as of January 1, 2008.

GROSS DOMESTIC PRODUCT (GDP)

$9.65 billion (2009 estimate)

GDP GROWTH

-4 percent (2009 estimate)

CURRENCY

Eurodollars (€)
US$1 = €0.73 (2010 estimate)

LAND USE

Arable land: 31.25 percent; permanent crops: 3.13 percent; others: 65.62 percent (2005 estimate)

AGRICULTURAL PRODUCTS

Potatoes, cauliflower, grapes, wheat, barley, tomatoes, citrus, cut flowers, green peppers, pork, milk, poultry, and eggs

MAJOR EXPORTS

Machinery and transportation equipment, manufactured and semi-manufactured goods

MAJOR IMPORTS

Machinery and transport equipment, manufactured and semi-manufactured goods, food, drink, tobacco

MAIN TRADE PARTNERS

Germany, Singapore, France, United States, United Kingdom, Hong Kong, Japan, Italy

WORKFORCE

171,000 (2008 estimate)

UNEMPLOYMENT RATE

6 percent (2009 estimate)

INFLATION

2.7 percent (2009 estimate)

EXTERNAL DEBT

$188.8 million (2005 estimate)

CULTURAL MALTA

Gantija
Gantija is a Neolithic age megalithic temple complex on Gozo. The Ggantija temples are the earliest of a series of megalithic temples in Malta. Together with other similar structures, the Megalithic Temples of Malta have been designated a UNESCO World Heritage Site

Manoel Theater
The Manoel Theater is reputed to be Europe's third-oldest working theater, and the oldest working theater in the Commonwealth of Nations. Located on Old Theater Street in Valletta, it is now Malta's National Theater and home to the Manoel Theater Museum.

The Mosta Dome
The Mosta Dome is a church in Mosta. Its dome is the third-largest church dome in Europe and the ninth-largest in the world, with a diameter of 122 feet (37 m). It was designed by the Maltese architect Giorgio Grognet.

National Museum of Archaeology
The National Museum of Archaeology in Valletta displays an exceptional array of artifacts from Malta's unique prehistoric periods, starting with the first arrival of humans in the Ghar Dalam phase (5200 B.C.) and running up to the Tarxien phase (2500 B.C.).

Ramla Bay
Situated on the tranquil isle of Gozo, this is an excellent unspoiled beach set in a beautiful valley. The color of the sand has given this beach its name, Ramla (il-Hamra), which literally means "red beach."

Saint John's Co-Cathedral and Museum
Saint John's Co-Cathedral and Museum was built as the temple of the Knights of Saint John. It is home to an impressive collection of art and artifacts, and is an important shrine and a sacred place of worship.

Saint Paul's Cathedral
Saint Paul's Cathedral is built on the site where governor Publius was reported to have met Saint Paul after his shipwreck off the Maltese coast. The cathedral has a substantial collection of silver plates and coins, and some carvings by the German artist Albrecht Dürer.

Mdina
Mdina, the old capital of Malta, is a medieval walled town situated on a hill in the center of the island. Much of its present architecture reflects the time of the Arab rulers of Malta until the Norman conquest of Malta in 1091 A.D.

Catacombs of Saint Paul and Saint Agatha
These catacombs in the town of Rabat were used in Roman times to bury the dead because, according to Roman culture, it was unclean to bury the dead in the city. Catacombs were also where early Christians secretly met and performed Mass.

Hypogeum
The Hypogeum in Paola, Malta, is a subterranean structure that became a necropolis in prehistoric times. Thought to have originally been a sanctuary, it is the only prehistoric underground temple in the world and became a UNESCO World Heritage Site in 1980.

Saluting Battery, Upper Barracca Gardens
The battery forms part of the city's old fortifications and provides gun salutes on national and religious festivals. It also used to mark time by firing at sunrise, midday, and sunset. There is a gorgeous view of Malta and the Grand Harbour from the battery.

Tarxien Temples
The Tarxien Temples are an archaeological complex in Tarxien, Malta. They date back to approximately 2800 B.C. Of particular interest at the temple site is the rich and intricate stonework, which includes depictions of domestic animals carved in altars.

OFFICIAL NAME
Republic of Malta

LAND AREA
122 square miles (316 square km)

CAPITAL
Valletta

MAJOR TOWNS
Birkirkara, Qormi, Mosta, Zabbar, Sliema

MAJOR ISLANDS
Malta, Gozo, Comino

HIGHEST POINT
Dingli Cliffs (829 feet/253 m)

POPULATION
405,165 (2009 estimate)

LIFE EXPECTANCY
Total population: 79.44 years
Male: 77.21 years
Female: 81.8 years (2009 estimate)

BIRTHRATE
10.36 births per 1,000 population (2009 estimate)

DEATH RATE
8.38 deaths per 1,000 population (2009 estimate)

ETHNIC GROUPS
Maltese (the descendants of ancient Carthaginians and Phoenicians with strong elements of Italian and other Mediterranean stock)

RELIGIONS
Roman Catholicism 98 percent, others 2 percent

MAIN LANGUAGES
Maltese (official) 90.2 percent, English (official) 6 percent, multilingual 3 percent, others 0.8 percent

MAIN POLITICAL PARTIES
Malta Labor Party
Nationalist Party

POLITICAL LEADERS
Dominic Mintoff—prime minister, 1955—58 and 1971—84; Karmenu Mifsud Bonnici—prime minister, 1984—87; Eddie Fenech Adami—prime minister, 1987—96, 1998—2004; president, 2004—present; Alfred Sant—prime minister, 1996—98; Lawrence Gonzi—prime minister, 2004—present

TIME LINE

IN MALTA	IN THE WORLD
720 B.C. A Greek colony is founded on Malta.	**753 B.C.** Rome is founded.
80 B.C. The islands come under the control of Carthage, a former Phoenician colony, and rapidly develop into a Carthaginian naval base.	
218 B.C. Invasion of Malta by the Roman Empire	
200 B.C. to A.D. 300 A Roman temple dedicated to the goddess Juno is built over the remains of the Tas-Sil megalithic temples.	
A.D. 41 The Maltese are granted municipal privileges by Rome.	**A.D. 600** Height of the Mayan civilization
870 Malta is conquered by Arabs, who introduce improved agricultural and irrigation systems.	**1000** The Chinese perfect gunpowder and begin to use it in warfare.
1091 Norman rule is established over Malta.	
1530 Emperor Charles V grants the Maltese Islands to the Knights of Saint John.	**1530** Beginning of transatlantic slave trade organized by the Portuguese in Africa
1798 Napoleon uses a ploy to seize the islands from the Knights.	
1799 Britain takes Malta under its protection.	
1814 Malta becomes a Crown colony of the British empire.	**1869** The Suez Canal is opened.
1934 English and Maltese are declared the official languages of Malta, and the Italian language is excluded.	**1914** World War I begins. **1939** World War II begins.
1942 King George VI awards the Malta colony the George Cross—Britain's highest civilian decoration—for heroism.	**1945** The United States drops atomic bombs on Hiroshima and Nagasaki, Japan. World War II ends.
1947 Self-government granted	

IN MALTA	IN THE WORLD
1959 Self-government revoked	
1962 Self-government restored	
1964 Full independence granted	
1971 Dom Mintoff's Malta Labor Party takes power.	
1974 Malta becomes a republic.	
1984 Mintoff resigns, succeeded by Carmelo Mifsud-Bonnici.	
	1986 Nuclear power disaster at Chernobyl in Ukraine
1987 Victory of Nationalist Party marks move toward European integration; Eddie Fenech-Adami becomes prime minister.	**1991** Breakup of the Soviet Union
1995 Malta joins NATO's Partnership for Peace program, only to leave in 1996	
1996 Labor Party, led by Alfred Sant, regains power	**1997** Hong Kong is returned to China.
1998 Eddie Fenech-Adami's Nationalist Party returns to power.	
1999 Guido de Marco is sworn in as president.	
2001 Pope John Paul II visits Malta and beatifies three Maltese clerics at an open-air ceremony.	**2001** Terrorists crash planes in New York, Washington, D.C., and Pennsylvania.
2003 Adami's ruling Nationalist Party claims victory in a general election.	**2003** War in Iraq begins.
2004 Lawrence Gonzi sworn in as prime minister following retirement of veteran leader Edward Fenech-Adami. Malta is one of 10 new states to join the EU.	
2008 Malta adopts the euro; During the March general elections, ruling Nationalist Party wins by a razor-thin margin.	**2008** The first black president of the United States, Barack Obama, is elected.

GLOSSARY

auberge
An inn of residence for the Knights of the Order of Saint John.

catacomb
An underground cemetery.

coralline
Composed of or having the structure of coral.

Eurozone
A currency union of European Union member states that have adopted the euro as their sole legal tender.

faqqus il-hmir (FAT-ous ill-hmeer)
Squirting cucumber, an unusual plant whose fruits explode when ripe.

figolla (FIG-ole-ar)
A pastry cut into various shapes, such as the Maltese Cross, prepared for Easter Sunday celebrations.

ghana (ANN-aa)
Poems that are sung to musical accompaniment.

gregale (grey-GAH-lay)
A cooling wind that blows in from the mountains in Italy.

hobz biz-zejt (hops BIZ-zeyt)
Maltese bread with olive oil.

kannoli (can-OH-lee)
A tube-shaped confection of deep-fried crisp pastry.

karozzin (ca-rotts-SEEN)
Horse-drawn carriage.

kusksu (kus-KSUE)
A traditional vegetable soup made from broad beans with pasta and tomatoes.

luzzijiet (LUT-tsie-yiet)
Traditional Maltese fishing boats.

megalithic
Structures made of large stones, utilizing an interlocking system without the use of mortar or cement.

mqarrun fil-forn (IM-ah-roon ill-fourn)
A traditional pasta-based dish.

necropolis
A prehistoric burial ground.

niccec (nee-chech)
Contribution boxes placed at shrines to the saints.

scirocco
A warm and sultry wind that blows across Malta from the Sahara at the beginning and end of each summer.

scree
A steep mass of broken rock on the side of a mountain.

Te Deum
A hymn of praise sung at a special service on the eve of a feast day.

FOR FURTHER INFORMATION

BOOKS

Aizpuricte, Amanda. *Malta New EU Countries and Citizens.* Burlington, Vermont: Cherrytree Books, 2005.

Aquilina, Joseph. *Concise Maltese—English—Maltese Dictionary.* Valletta, Malta: Midsea Books, 2006.

Badger, George Percy. *Historical Guide to Malta and Gozo.* Boston: Adamant Media Corporation, 2005.

Bain, Carolyn. *Malta and Gozo* (Country Guide). Melbourne: Lonely Planet, 2007.

Correggio, Francisco Balbi di. *The Siege of Malta, 1565* (First Person Singular). Suffolk: Boydell Press, 2005.

Crowley, Roger. *Empires of the Sea: The Siege of Malta, the Battle of Lepanto, and the Contest for the Center of the World.* New York: Random House Trade Paperbacks, 2009.

Mamo, S. *English-Maltese Dictionary.* Bilingual edition. Charleston, SC: BiblioLife, 2009.

Porter, Whitworth. *A History of the Knights of Malta: or, The Order of St. John of Jerusalem.* Charleston, SC: BiblioLife, 2009.

Stafford, James. *Malta* (The European Union: Political, Social, and Economic Cooperation). Broomall, PA: Mason Crest Publishers, 2005.

FILMS

Global Treasures Prehistoric Malta. TravelVideoStore.com, 2007.

Historic Encounters: Against All Odds. Goldhill Home Media, 2008.

Seven Days: Malta. TravelVideoStore.com, 2007.

MUSIC

Malta with Siena Wind Orchestra. *Colezo! Malta.* Jvc Victor, 2005.

Malta with Siena Wind Orchestra. *Manhattan in Blue.* Jvc Victor, 2004.

Various artists. *Time in Malta: Alone with the Alone.* Equal Vision Records, 2004.

WEBSITES

CIA World Factbook: Malta. www.cia.gov/library/publications/the-world-factbook/geos/mt.html

Malta.com: The Essential Guide to the Maltese Islands. www.malta.com/

Malta National Statistics Office. www.nso.gov.mt/site/page.aspx

Visit Malta: The Official Tourism Site for Malta, Gozo, and Comino. www.visitmalta.com/main

BIBLIOGRAPHY

BOOKS

Balm, Roger. *Malta* (American Geographical Society Around the World Program). Granville, OH: McDonald & Woodward Pub Co., 1996.

Bonello, Giovanni. *Histories of Malta Volume 7: Closures and Disclosures*. Valletta, Malta: Midsea Books, 2006

Borg, Victor Paul. *Malta and Gozo* (Rough Guide Directions). London: Rough Guides, 2008.

DK Publishing. *Top 10 Malta and Gozo* (Eyewitness Top 10 Travel Guide). London: DK Travel, 2009.

Editors of Time Out. *Time Out Shortlist Malta.* London: Time Out, 2008.

Levy, Pat. *Essential Malta and Gozo.* London: AA Publications, 2005.

Pickles, Tim. *Malta 1565: Last Battle of the Crusades.* Mechanicsburg, PA: Stackpole Books, 1998.

Porter, Whitworth. *A History of the Fortress of Malta.* Charleston, SC: Bibliolife, 2009.

Richards, Brian. *Malta* (Globetrotter Travel Packs). London: New Holldand Publishing, 2008.

Rose, Lesley Anne. *Malta and Gozo* (Frommer's Day By Day Series). Hoboken, NJ: John Wiley & Sons, Inc., 2009.

Seth, Ronald. *Let's Visit Malta.* London: Burke Publishing, 1985.

Shores, Christopher, Cull, Brian, & Malizia, *Malta: The Hurricane Years*. Nicola. London: Grub Street Publishing, 1992.

Sire, H.J.A. *The Knights of Malta.* New Haven, CT: Yale University Press, 1996.

Stephenson, Charles and Noon, Steve. *The Fortifications of Malta 1530—1945* (Fortress). Valletta, Malta: Osprey Publishing, 2004.

WEBSITES

About Malta—History. www.aboutmalta.com/

Absolute Astronomy—Malta. www.absoluteastronomy.com/timeline/Malta

Encyclopedia of the Nations—Malta. www.nationsencyclopedia.com/Europe/Malta

Gvern Ta' Malta. www.gov.mt

Hill Museumand Manuscript Library. www.hmml.org

iexplore—Malta. www.iexplore.com/dmap/Malta/History

Infoplease—Malta. www.infoplease.com/ipa/A0107763.html

Jewish International Library—Malta. www.jewishvirtuallibrary.org/jsource/vjw/Malta.html

Legal-Malta. www.legal-malta.com

Malta. www.malta.com

Malta History and Archaeology. www.maltahistory.org.uk

National Statistics Office Malta. www.nso.gov.mt/site/page.aspx

Times of Malta. www.timesofmalta.com

Visit Malta. www.visitmalta.com

INDEX

INDEX